"With empowering and compassionate languag[e] [the]re's a comprehensive resource that is an absolute lifeline to teens. The authors seamlessly bridge the gap between thought and action, offering gentle exploration and practical strategies to handle tough times. Reading this guide is like settling in with a wonderfully affirming loved one that sees you for all of your magic and worth. An absolute must-have on your bookshelf—these words are gold."

    —**Rachel E. Simon, LCSW, MEd**, psychotherapist, educator, and author of *The Every Body Book* and *The Every Body Book of Consent*

"*The Trans and Gender Diverse Teen Resilience Guide* is an empowering resource for teens who are navigating life as their authentic selves in a world that too often challenges their existence. With practical tools for self-compassion, coping, and building a sense of belonging, this guide helps teens create a life worth living, even when times are hard. A must-read for fostering strength, safety, and joy amidst adversity."

    —**Dara Hoffman, LPC**, author of *You and Your Gender Identity*

"*The Trans and Gender Diverse Teen Resilience Guide* provides young people with a brilliant extra tool in their toolbox to navigate the challenges the teen years bring. Although primarily a resource for adolescents, those parenting and working with trans and gender diverse teens will gain beneficial insight into these challenges, and potentially increase empathy and understanding regarding ways they can support the young person in their lives."

    —**Jo Hirst**, author of *A House for Everyone*

the *instant help* solutions series

Young people today need mental health resources more than ever. That's why New Harbinger created the **Instant Help Solutions Series** especially for teens. Written by leading psychologists, physicians, and professionals, these evidence-based self-help books offer practical tips and strategies for dealing with a variety of mental health issues and life challenges teens face, such as depression, anxiety, bullying, eating disorders, trauma, and self-esteem problems.

Studies have shown that young people who learn healthy coping skills early on are better able to navigate problems later in life. Engaging and easy-to-use, these books provide teens with the tools they need to thrive—at home, at school, and on into adulthood.

This series is part of the **New Harbinger Instant Help Books** imprint, founded by renowned child psychologist Lawrence Shapiro. For a complete list of books in this series, visit newharbinger.com.

THE TRANS & GENDER DIVERSE TEEN RESILIENCE GUIDE

Essential Skills for Building Community, Well-Being & Mental Health

JAYME L. PETA, PHD
DEB COOLHART, PHD
RYLAN JAY TESTA, PHD

Instant Help Books
An Imprint of New Harbinger Publications, Inc.

Publisher's Note

This publication is designed to provide accurate and authoritative information in regard to the subject matter covered. It is sold with the understanding that the publisher is not engaged in rendering psychological, financial, legal, or other professional services. If expert assistance or counseling is needed, the services of a competent professional should be sought.

INSTANT HELP, the Clock Logo, and NEW HARBINGER are trademarks of New Harbinger Publications, Inc.

New Harbinger Publications is an employee-owned company.

Copyright © 2025 by Jayme L. Peta, Deborah Coolhart, and Rylan Jay Testa
Instant Help Books
An imprint of New Harbinger Publications, Inc.
5720 Shattuck Avenue
Oakland, CA 94609
www.newharbinger.com

All Rights Reserved

Cover design by Sara Christian

Acquired by Wendy Millstine and Ryan Buresh

Edited by Karen Schader

Library of Congress Cataloging-in-Publication Data on file

MIX
Paper | Supporting responsible forestry
FSC
www.fsc.org
FSC® C008955

Printed in the United States of America

27   26   25

10   9   8   7   6   5   4   3   2   1   First Printing

We dedicate this book to transgender, nonbinary, and gender diverse youth. You're finding your way through an especially challenging world, and we want you to know that we see you, hear you, respect you, and celebrate you. We know that, even though you're under attack, you're valid, lovable, courageous, compassionate, beautiful, creative, gifted, rebellious, strong, socially aware, bold, flexible, silly, and wise. Just by existing, you're contributing to making the world a kinder, more colorful, and safer place for all.

We also dedicate this book to Dr. Peter Goldblum, Dr. Kimberly Balsam, and our other mentors, as well as our parents, families, and chosen families. In a way, our squads wrote this book and taught us that in community is resilience, and in resilience, community.

TABLE OF CONTENTS

INTRODUCTION

No matter how you identify your gender, we've written this book like we were writing to a really good friend. We're here to encourage you, to remind you that you're a person who deserves care and friends and the chance to make a great life. Helping you find ways to accept yourself, feel better, and take excellent care of yourself is our mission because we know that the world needs you, even though it doesn't always treat people like you that well. We're so glad to meet you and join you on this journey.

We know that other people might also pick up this book: parents, teachers, therapists, friends, siblings, and curious people might all want to read a book about how trans, nonbinary, and gender diverse youth can become more resilient. To these people, we say that, although we didn't write this book for you, we're so grateful you're here. These youth need a lot of people to join them on their journey toward a powerful, meaningful life. Welcome.

MEET THE AUTHORS

Jayme Peta: Jayme is a nonbinary psychologist who teaches new therapists about how to help LGBTQ+ youth and adults. Jayme also oversees clinical training for doctoral students at the Wright Institute. Jayme has found that building supportive community has helped so much at even the hardest times. The squad is everything! Jayme feels best when getting enough exercise, sunshine, and time with plants. Hiking in the East Bay of the San Francisco area is a sure way to get all three.

Rylan Jay Testa: Ry is a trans man who transitioned about fifteen years ago. He's a psychologist who has done work to support the mental health of trans, nonbinary, and gender diverse adults and teens. Ry has done research to see how minority stressors affect trans, nonbinary, and gender diverse people, and how they are able to be resilient. He has worked as a professor and a therapist. Ry knows that everyone has their own things that help them feel safe, happy, and that they belong. Ry feels these things when he's outdoors in nature, when he's with birds, when he's with close friends and family, when he takes a hot shower, when he listens to calm or happy music, and when he plays music with other people.

Deb Coolhart: Deb is a queer cis female therapist who has specialized in providing gender-affirmative care for trans youth and their families for twenty-five years. She's also a professor of Marriage and Family Therapy at Syracuse University, where she created the Transgender Affirmative Support Team twenty years ago. This team provides gender-affirming therapy and engages in local activism to support the trans and gender diverse community. Working alongside trans youth, she has built a solid practice of self-care to strengthen her resilience in fighting for trans rights. To recharge, she loves to spend time with her best friends…belly laughing is healing! To express her frustration and anger about injustice and mistreatment, she does kickboxing regularly; safely punching and kicking things can feel like a release. For calm and comfort, she loves to cuddle with her three dogs, Buddy, Cinnamon, and Nova, all of whom have come to every author meeting. And for spiritual connection to all life, she loves nature and especially planting vegetables, herbs, and flowers, and watching them grow.

MEET THE YOUTH

To help us understand what resilience means to trans and gender diverse teens, we talked a lot with four trans and/or nonbinary youth—Criella, Louis, Jade, and Rowan—who volunteered to be interviewed and share their thoughts and experiences building resilience. Through them, we learned a lot about the challenges these teens face and what they have done to stay well. You'll be reading their real stories throughout this book, though they each have used a pseudonym to protect their privacy.

Criella identifies as a trans woman and came out when she was fourteen. She experienced a lot of challenges with friends and school bullying. In her pursuit of resilience, Criella likes to process difficulties with her partners, do goth makeup, create art, explore herbal teas and their benefits, and hike.

Louis identifies as transmasculine and nonbinary, and his pronouns are he/him. He came out as trans when he was thirteen, and his biggest challenge was that it took a couple of years for his parents to accept his identity, delaying his access to gender-affirming medical care. To get through tough times, Louis likes to draw, listen to music, watch animated shows, and paint his nails.

Jade had expressed herself in a feminine way her whole life, but figured out that she was actually a trans girl when she was eleven. Jade's school and community environments were her biggest challenges, as she was living in a politically conservative rural area. To get through challenges, Jade likes to talk to trusted friends and family members, cuddle with her dog, take bubble baths, read, crochet, bake, hula hoop—and scream into a pillow when all else fails!

Rowan identifies as a trans male and came out at age seventeen. He has experienced challenges in his family, school, and work environments as a result of his gender identity. To manage difficult emotions and mistreatment, Rowan likes to journal, play guitar, listen to music, dance, ride his skateboard, and work on his car.

All of these youth have faced significant challenges in their journeys with gender and have grown to develop self-compassion, more comfort with their bodies, self-care practices, positive coping, community, and meaning in their lives, ultimately resulting in their resilience. We thank them for sharing their wisdom with us all!

MEETING YOU

You've met the authors, you've met the youth. Now it's time for us to meet you! You might be wondering, *Is this book for me?* We wrote this book for any young person who identifies—or thinks they might identify—as transgender or gender nonbinary or gender diverse. All this means is that, in some way, you don't feel that your gender—your feeling of being a girl or boy, or both or neither—doesn't match the one everyone thought you'd be. There are lots of words for this; some might fit you and some might not. We use the term "trans and gender diverse" (TGD) to talk about anyone who has had the experience that their gender doesn't match what they were told (or wonders if this might be true). This includes all kinds of identities, like nonbinary, agender and so on, and you can be sure that if we met in real life, we'd use whatever word you like.

HOW THIS BOOK WORKS

This book is designed to walk you through the steps to creating your own personal pathway to building the life you really want. We'll be recommending that you write, draw, or think about things along the way, and it will be helpful to have one place where you keep all your resilience tools to pull out whenever you need them. We strongly recommend that you use a journal. It can contain anything you want—you can include art, writing, pictures. You can use your phone as a journal with video or audio recordings and notes. Do what works for you.

It will be up to you to decide how much of this you want to do, what parts work and don't work for you, and what the right pathway is. There is no one way to work on becoming more resilient. What works is *what works for you*. Afro-Cuban trans youth activist Grace Dolan-Sandrino (2017) writes, "Trans people are extraordinary, strong, intelligent, persistent and resilient. We have to be." To us that means you have courage, smarts, and resilience already in you. This book is about finding those strengths and feeding them to be stronger and more accessible.

To start, we first need to understand what resilience is. In the first chapter, we'll talk about some different meanings of resilience and why it's important to think of it as an action you do with community rather than a way of being. We will also discuss how resilience can be part of resistance and changing the world—or at least, your world—for the better. This will create a foundation for discussing how to cultivate a sense of strength and resilience in your life.

We'll start chapter 2 by talking about developing self-compassion. Until we find our way back to feeling that we really do deserve good things, it's hard to take bigger steps toward bouncing forward. Discrimination, negative messages, bullying, and *gender dysphoria* (experiencing discomfort with one's body) can all lead to shame and discomfort within yourself. We'll go over some simple ways to reclaim your right to be kind to yourself.

This project can be very hard when you're experiencing a lot of sadness or frustration with your body, as TGD people often do. Criella takes hormones that help with her dysphoria, but it also surfaces when people use the wrong name or pronoun for her or when she's feeling unhappy with her voice. So we wrote chapter 3 on how to make friends with your body. Reconnecting with our bodies is a powerful way to increase your acceptance of yourself. Criella shares: "For a while, I wanted to change my voice because I thought that would make people stop misgendering me, which it might, but maybe that's not the point. Maybe the point of being trans is to be who you are for you." Accepting and loving your body—even as you're considering changes—can be a huge challenge but comes with some huge rewards, like feeling more content, more accepting, and more at home with yourself.

Starting to experience self-compassion and self-acceptance means that the next step is learning how to treat yourself like someone who deserves love and happiness. Chapter 4 is about taking good care of yourself mentally and physically. Self-care can be so hard when you're experiencing dysphoria, anxiety, or depression, or have gotten many negative messages about yourself, so we will work through simple ways to help overcome some of those obstacles. Criella uses fashion to give herself new positive messages about how she looks, while reminding herself that she can just enjoy life: "I enjoy the extravagance you can put into feminine presentation and just having fun with that, like not taking it too seriously, just being experimental, and trying to grow your style." Self-care can look like a lot of things, including helping you feel good about yourself and spending more time just enjoying life. After all, in a world that doesn't always see TGD people as worthy of care or fun, taking good care of yourself is really the ultimate TGD activism. Every time we treat ourselves well, and help others do the same, it's one more blow against the anti-trans forces of the world!

Regardless of how much self-compassion you develop and self-care you do, you may still experience hard times, so chapter 5 will cover what to do when big life challenges happen. How do you bounce forward when you get hit with intense dysphoria at school or your boss misgenders you…again? We'll talk about what you can do in the toughest moments to make sure you get through them safely and can return to a better state. These are skills you can also use to help friends and people in your community who are having their own tough time.

Chapter 6 is devoted to finding a community of supportive people that you also support. Criella describes this process: "Just trying to be a good friend, a good partner, good for everyone who wants you there, you know? Just being kind and supportive. Because then it comes back. Like, if you're kind to others, then chances are, they'll be kind back to you. Like you're learning to be kind to someone and they're learning to be kind to someone and so then you can transfer it to being kind to yourself."

Research backs up Criella's wisdom: TGD youth are happier and healthier when they're able to connect with other queer and trans communities (Paceley et al. 2021). So, the next focus of this chapter will be thinking through how you want to create your community: the people who will make up your system of support and who you also support. Getting through tough times is not something people need to do by themselves (even if we get a lot of messages saying not to ask for help).

In the final chapter, on building a meaningful life, we will look at the ways that TGD youth can turn resilience into resistance and meaning. Self-advocacy, activism, and connecting with community can be powerful ways to not only survive your environment but also build the life you'll want in the future. Criella makes the point that part of building a better life for herself has involved finding her own values, including "rejecting the social norms I was taught. Queerness, to me, means resistance against society's negative norms. We should be pushing the envelope." Research shows that TGD youth and adults often state that activism and self-advocacy have helped them stay hopeful, feel powerful, and actually make their schools, workplaces, neighborhoods, and communities better for future TGD people (Breslow et al. 2015; Singh 2013). While we strongly feel that the responsibility should not be on trans youth to make things better, we also know that as humans, learning to advocate for ourselves, resist discrimination and negative messages, and uplift our loved ones can be such an important source of strength.

Part of that, too, is finding other areas of meaning in the resistance against *transphobia* (dislike or discrimination against TGD people). No one should have to struggle or experience dysphoria, transphobia, racism, and so on. And for those who do experience it, finding meaning, connection, spirituality, creativity, and more through this struggle can be an important factor in feeling hopeful and happy. In fact, recent studies have shown that people who report growing stronger after experiencing trauma say that it was because they found powerful meaning in their recovery (Tedeschi and Calhoun 2004). Regardless of your experience, we believe that it's not enough just to survive. No one wakes up every morning eager to be resilient to another misgendering. We need to find a life worth living. This, we think, is your birthright, and whatever else you take away from this book, we hope you take away that you deserve to build a meaningful life.

At the end you'll find a section with resources for dealing with crisis. Many other resources will be found at http://www.newharbinger.com/54193, our free tools webpage. There is also a helpful glossary with definitions of the words that may be unfamiliar to you.

These chapters are written to be read in order but also to be read at your own pace. We encourage you to skim or skip what doesn't work. Take time to try things out and digest a chapter before moving on. Or, if you find that a chapter feels overwhelming, go back to an earlier chapter and see if exercises or ideas there appeal to you more. This is your journey, so take what you want, leave what you don't. We're just glad to come along with you.

CHAPTER I

WHAT IS
RESILIENCE?

We wrote this book because we think that resilience is one of the most important things for transgender, nonbinary, and gender diverse youth (any person who doesn't identify with the gender of "male" or "female" that they were probably assumed to be at birth) to know about, and to learn how to develop for themselves. But what do we mean by resilience? One definition that people use is that resilience is the ability to bounce back from difficult life circumstances. Obviously, being more resilient seems like a good idea, but a lot of people have criticisms of this view, asking, "Bounce back to what?" and "Why should I try to be happy when so many things are wrong?" Or even, "Why should I have to be responsible for developing resilience? I didn't make the world the hard place that it is!" These are important criticisms, and you'll find that our definition of resilience might be a little different.

We'll start with Criella, who helped us introduce this book and will explain what resilience is. She's a seventeen-year-old trans woman who works hard at staying not just strong, but really fierce in becoming who she wants to be.

To, us, resilience means having as good a life as possible, even when things are hard. After all, people are not squishy balls that bounce back to the same shape they were before something hard happened. Criella helped us understand this by saying: "You often hear a lot of trans people saying they don't expect to make it to eighteen. So maybe resilience is the step of having a future image. Trying to keep going because you can still hold that image in your mind." Her words reminded us that people grow and change, and holding on for a different future is an important part of resilience. In fact, many people say that they feel changed—often for the better—after coming out as TGD, even though it was hard. They didn't bounce back; instead they bounced forward (Manyena et al. 2011). Sometimes discussions of resilience seem to be saying that you should stay happy and optimistic, and that as long as you're doing well in school or at work, you're resilient.

We disagree with this and want to point out that we all have plenty in our lives to feel unhappy, angry, and uncomfortable with. Sometimes people aren't doing well in school or at work because they find they don't fit well in the school or work systems, or are busy doing things to take care of themselves, or even doing things that keep them alive. Looking happy and successful is not the point. Finding a life worth living is. Still others point out that they didn't find ways to make a good life on their own, but by finding a supportive, caring community. We agree that community support is important, and you'll read more about this later in the book. But finding the right community can take some time, so this book is written to help you have as good a life as possible, given how your life is right now, and it can also support you in eventually finding your community, being a part of change you believe in, and ultimately figuring out what shape you want to bounce into next.

WHY IS IT SO HARD TO BOUNCE FORWARD?

Through no fault of their own, many people experience difficult life situations, such as trauma, growing up in poverty, racism or other discrimination, not having health care, and more. These difficult situations influence how they think and feel about themselves and others, to the point where their mental health starts to worsen.

And, the more difficult life experiences you have, the harder it gets to find ways to feel good and healthy. Most people who experience many difficult life experiences start to think negatively about themselves, to feel depressed and hopeless about the future. Those negative ways of thinking and feeling make it even harder to feel okay when new bad things happen. It's a negative spiral to feeling worse and worse. In short, the more life knocks you around, the harder it is to get up, let alone bounce. Criella told us: "There was a time when I didn't know what the future image looked like, and I was depressed. I didn't think I would make it." When hard things happen, it's hard to even imagine that there is something to hold on for.

Life can knock transgender and gender diverse youth around *a lot.* In addition to the challenges we named above, gender dysphoria and growing up in an environment where TGD people are being increasingly targeted by some political leaders all reduce resiliency.

Luckily, we have a lot of experience helping people become more resilient. And we've also had a lot of experience putting our research into action to help TGD people boost their resilience even when they're experiencing anxiety, depression, and other tough situations as a result. This book is about helping you put into action all of what we've learned—and what we learned from Criella, Louis, Rowan, and Jade—about staying strong and healthy.

CHALLENGES FACING TGD YOUTH

As you probably know, many TGD youth experience family rejection, bullying, trouble getting health care, and other forms of discrimination and harm. Even if you haven't experienced discrimination or violence, you've probably heard of TGD people experiencing them. The fact that our culture discriminates against TGD people is part of what causes *minority stress,* which is the stress people experience due to being rejected by society, discriminated against, or experiencing violence as a result of their identity. Two of your authors, Ry and Jayme, have researched minority stress in transgender and nonbinary (genders that are not just "man" or "woman") people and have been able to show that the extra stress of being a TGD person causes a lot more anxiety, depression, and even suicidal thinking. And worse, experiencing discrimination, rejection, and violence leads to thoughts and feelings of shame about being TGD. We call this *internalized transphobia.* This is the way that the ugly messages about being TGD from our culture get under your skin and make TGD people start to think that it's their fault that bad things happen, or to have negative thoughts about themselves. Throughout this book, we'll be explaining how this happens and helping you find ways to stop repeating these harmful messages to yourself.

The same stress can happen for people of color; lesbian, gay, bisexual, and queer people; people with disabilities; immigrants; neurodivergent people, and others. Youth who have multiple oppressed (or marginalized) identities also have minority stress related to those identities. Those different stresses build up and interact with each other, making it even harder to stay happy and well. It's hard to find community, look forward to things, or even think of yourself as a good person when everyone else is telling you that you're bad or wrong, crazy or broken.

We know that there are ways to increase resilience to these hardships, but that doesn't mean just making yourself feel happy and joyful all the time. That's not realistic. It means when times are tough, you can rebuild, and sometimes rebuild even stronger. While our book can't change your family, school, work, or body, it can help you tap into your strengths and smarts to help you live a better life. We feel strongly that helping TGD youth who have experienced a lot of struggle, pain, discrimination, or adversity learn ways to get and stay strong, find community, and be well is essential.

WHAT DO WE KNOW ABOUT RESILIENCE?

In the 1970s, when US researchers first began to explore what helps some people thrive after difficult life experiences, they started by identifying personality traits. Of course, a lot of this research was done on upper-class cisgender white men. And, while personality traits are helpful to know, it's not all that easy to change one's personality. However, other researchers soon began to see the value of looking into aspects beyond personality and also discovering that there are things people can do not just to survive tough times, but to be strong. These ideas were researched more in people with different kinds of difficult life experiences, and in a much wider diversity of humans—youth, people of color, women, transgender people, LGB people, people with disabilities, immigrants, and more. We looked at all of this research to help us write this book.

To understand what these researchers learned, let's think about that popular school experiment some of you may have done, where you try to build different structures around an egg to protect it in a fall. Perhaps one person tried surrounding the egg with bubble wrap, and someone else used rubber bands to suspend the egg inside a ball. Then the classes do experiments to see how the eggs fare when they're all dropped from a height. From a short distance, and landing on, say, soft grass, most eggs are going to be okay. Maybe they'll have a little crack but they'll stay whole. But, if the egg has been through some previous falls or had cracks from other events, well, it's more likely to break. The regular old eggshell works well to protect the egg, but the more it gets cracked, the harder it is for that egg to stay strong. To help us think about resilience, let's say the egg is like a person. Resilience researchers started to ask: what makes one human-egg break while another stays intact under the same circumstances?

The first researchers, as we said, looked at personality. So, basically some eggs have shells that are thicker or tougher. This is good to know. This is an important factor. Some of us are born with personalities that are just kind of tough. Things like your commitment to yourself, finding meaning in life, being optimistic, or being oriented toward growing are all traits that help people stay resilient. And some of us are more sensitive or aren't as optimistic. That's just how we are, and it's not our fault. But an egg can't do much to get a tougher shell when it's just an egg! We can do *some* things to change our personality but not so much.

But what if you changed the environment? This is the next area that researchers investigated. They learned that when people go through rough life events—for example, experiencing trauma or discrimination—they have more resilience if they have a supportive environment. The environment is something you could change in the egg experiment. For example, can you give the egg a better environment by building a little structure around it so it'll bounce and not break? Can you give the egg more social support by giving it a softer place to land? These things also seem to work and are good to know. When we want to help people bounce forward, we need to help them have a better environment, like warm, supportive families, community, good teachers, health care, and therapy. That way, when things get hard, your environment protects you and helps you rebuild your "shell."

But still, an egg is just an egg, and what you just read might leave you wondering about how you're supposed to be more resilient if you have to wait around for someone to build a more supportive environment for you. This is an important critique of a lot of talk about resilience: that TGD youth should not have to just cope with invalidation from family or others (ignoring your gender identity or not taking it seriously), discrimination, bullying, and so on. It's not fair, and instead we should work on changing our culture to make it more supportive. Of course this is true…but in the meantime, what can you do?

This question leads us to the next and most exciting research: that TGD youth are actually happier and healthier and do better when they get to be an active part of not only developing their own strengths but also building their own communities, and for many people, making a difference for those around them. This is bouncing forward—finding your own ways to change your life to survive hard times and, eventually, make the life you want.

It turns out that a huge factor in resilience is what a person can do for themselves and in their environment, such as school, work, or neighborhoods. You don't have to wait around like an egg for someone to build a safe structure; you have a remarkable ability to change, grow, advocate, and get what you need. To really understand resilience, we need to think of people not as eggs but as humans who are able to grow, build skills in dealing with difficult circumstances, and best of all, join with other people to make communities. And, for many people, to advocate for themselves and their communities.

These abilities are especially important for TGD youth and youth of color. You can create support for yourself and increase your resilience by, for example, finding positive friendships or great mentors. Despite your struggles, you can do a lot to strengthen yourself, find your own support, and make your schools, neighborhoods, and lives better. Research shows that TGD youth who make meaning of their experiences through advocacy, activism, or just helping their community are more likely to bounce forward (Paceley et al. 2021). TGD youth of color who find connections in communities where they can feel proud of their culture and community are more able to remain happy and healthy overall (Singh 2013). When you learn to appreciate, accept, and most of all, love yourself, you're more likely to grow and get stronger even when faced with tough stuff.

RESISTANCE AND RESILIENCE

Our approach to resilience is about being active in becoming stronger for yourself and also for your community. Often this comes in the form of advocating for your community and resisting anti-trans discrimination. Miss Major Griffin-Gracy, a Black trans author and activist, put all of this together when she said, "I want you to train and teach and love on and create families within my community...so that we can understand that we have a culture, we have a history, we have a reason to be here. We have a purpose. We're entitled to be loved, and seek happiness, and share that with the people that we care about" (Drucker 2018). Miss Major emphasizes how important it is to take an active part in creating your own resilience: that self-love, creating a caring community, and finding pride and purpose in a TGD community are all so important to being happy and healthy but also require resistance to all the factors that we know harm TGD youth.

A NOTE ON SAFETY

Part of resilience is staying alive and feeling as good as possible until you can do even more to make your life worth living. Sometimes, all the support in the world isn't enough to make you feel safe and well. Depression, anxiety, and thoughts about suicide are pretty common for people who are facing big life challenges, being mistreated, or dealing with depression. Having these thoughts and feelings doesn't mean you're bad, weak, or not resilient. In fact, a key part of bouncing forward is knowing when to reach outside yourself for support.

We recommend that all TGD youth who are experiencing mental health problems or serious problems at home, school, or work, or struggling with their identity seek a gender-affirming therapist or counselor for help, or at least alert a supportive adult that you need help. Don't go it alone if you're experiencing any of these:

- Family rejection or abuse
- Bullying or harassment
- Sexual assault or sexual abuse
- Violence

- Feeling confused and upset about your gender identity or sexual orientation

- Being told that you need to change your gender identity or sexual orientation

Here are some other red flags that may mean you need to reach out for more help: feeling intense depression, anxiety, or dysphoria that feels unmanageable. By unmanageable, we mean that these feelings are getting in the way of your regular life (going to school, taking care of your body, connecting with others). Other flags are not being able to do things you used to enjoy, having intense sleep problems, gaining or losing a lot of weight, having trouble with eating, or engaging in self-harm behaviors. If any of these are happening for you, it's important that you seek help. Good places to start are a school counselor, a therapist, or other trusted adults.

If you're having suicidal thoughts, one way to monitor the danger of these thoughts is to understand the difference between passive and active suicidal thoughts. Passive suicidal thoughts sound like *I wish I weren't here*, or *I hope I don't wake up tomorrow*, or *I just can't take it anymore*. Passive suicidal thoughts tend to focus on wanting the pain to end without a direct intention to die. Passive suicidal thoughts should be taken seriously, as they can sometimes become active, and you should definitely talk to someone supportive about them as soon as you can.

Active suicidal thoughts are when you're thinking about how you would die and coming up with a plan for how you would end your life. These thoughts are very serious and are one of those red flags telling you to seek help quickly. If you feel like you're in immediate danger of acting on your suicidal thoughts, go immediately to a hospital, or contact the Trevor Project. The Trevor Project is especially for LGBTQ+ (lesbian, gay, bisexual, transgender, queer, questioning and more) youth, and is staffed 24/7. You can text them at 678678; call them at 1-866-488-7386; or chat with them online at https://www.thetrevorproject.org/get-help. We strongly recommend that you go to the Trevor Project page even if you're feeling great. Even if you don't need their resources and information, you may have a friend who does. Save their number in your phone or write it in your journal right now so you have it when you need it.

Another important resource is the Trans Lifeline. This is a hotline staffed by trans/nonbinary people who are there to talk, even if you're not in a crisis; call (877) 565-8860. They aren't available 24/7, but they have great resources on their page: https://translifeline.org/. Look in our resources section toward the back of this book to find this information in a hurry. These and a lot of other resources are also available in our free online tools at http://www.newharbinger.com/54193.

TAKEAWAYS

* Resilience is not just acting like hard times don't matter or like things are great all the time; it's also about having as good a life as possible, even when things are hard.

* People who experience discrimination have minority stress; that is, negative messages from the world that get under your skin and start to impact how you think about yourself, your identity, and your life. It's not your fault, and there are ways to undo these messages.

* TGD youth who are actively building their own strength, resilience, and communities are happier and healthier. We call this bouncing forward to building a new and better life, while making things as good as possible in the moment.

* Staying alive and well is the most important thing you can be doing right now. We list crisis lines that you should make use of if you ever feel in danger of suicide. We recommend that you find a gender-affirming therapist to work with if you're experiencing depression, anxiety, or other mental health concerns. If you're feeling suicidal, contact a crisis line or alert a trusted adult right away. Crisis lines are listed in the resources section at the back of the book.

* We recommend using some kind of journal to create your own resilience toolkit to refer to and build on.

CHAPTER 2

SELF-COMPASSION IN A HARD WORLD

The first step we're taking on this journey together is focused on self-compassion because we believe it's the most powerful foundation for building resilience. And we're not the only ones who think so! Recently, many authors, thinkers, and researchers have shown that people—including LGBTQ youth—who have more self-compassion are better able to bounce forward after hard times than those who tend to be self-critical (Neff and McGehee 2009; Vigna, Poehlmann-Tynan, and Koenig 2018).

As a TGD youth, you're at particularly high risk for hearing negative messages from others, over and above the negative messages that most people hear. Bullying, rejection, and dysphoria can all lead you to thinking very harsh thoughts about yourself. Add in negative messages about your race, size, background, and more, and it's easy to see how you might have internalized some of these messages and started to believe them about yourself. This is what we referred to in chapter 1 as internalized transphobia. And, yes, this is exactly how many TGD youth, youth of color, youth with larger body sizes, and others come to be more depressed and anxious—they start to *believe* the negative messages they have heard. It is not your fault if you have started to believe these messages, and this book is going to help you explore ways you can unlearn them. Self-compassion is one of the most important tools for unlearning messages of self-harshness and self-criticism and learning a new way to think about yourself: with acceptance and kindness.

The skills you'll learn in this chapter will give you a foundation for the skills in the rest of this book. Treating yourself with compassion is the starting place for finding meaning, hope, and encouragement when life is hard. And the more compassion you have for yourself, the more able you are to move toward what you really want in life After all, the negative messages you tell yourself came from outside you, and the best way to change the script is to look within yourself.

Many people hear about self-compassion and want to skip ahead to work on something else because it sounds uncomfortable. We would like to encourage you to stay with us in this chapter even if it's a little uncomfortable. You might feel uneasy because you have come to believe that being nice to yourself is not for you. But it is, and we'll help you understand why.

Think about the people in your life you care about deeply. You probably feel they deserve acceptance, kindness, patience, and encouragement. When your friend is being hard on themselves because they did poorly on a test, or their partner is mad at them, you probably say things like "But that test was really hard" or "It's not all your fault" or even "Don't be so hard on yourself." In fact, it often feels *painful* to see your friends be unkind to themselves. So why do they deserve this kindness, but somehow, you don't?

WHAT IS SELF-COMPASSION?

Many refer to this concept as self-love. It's the idea that we can turn the love, reassurance, and acceptance we offer to loved friends and family back toward ourselves. Self-compassion includes thinking and responding to ourselves and our thoughts in a gentle, forgiving, helpful, and accepting way. It means accepting *all* the parts of ourselves, including the parts we really don't like. It means that when we're having a hard time, we offer ourselves comfort instead of harsh judgment. Or when we fail at something, we encourage ourselves instead of being mean.

A lot of writing and thinking about self-compassion comes from Buddhist teachings. In those teachings, the idea is that as we learn to be more compassionate in the world, we must include ourselves and all the parts of ourselves. Some of the most powerful teachings include instructions to look at our suffering in the way a loving adult might help a baby. Buddhist teacher and activist Thich Nhat Hanh (2010) said: "It's like a mother when the baby is crying. Your anxiety is your baby. You have to take care of it. You have to go back to yourself, recognize the suffering in you, embrace the suffering, and you get relief."

Thich Nhat Hanh reminds us that self-compassion means not turning away from our suffering, not being mean to ourselves, but taking care of ourselves when we're having a hard time. Many of us were taught the opposite of this: that if we're going to be better or do better, we need to criticize, judge, or disrespect ourselves. We've all heard "Don't be a baby," for example, when we're upset or crying. Or that we need to "get it together," "grow up," or "don't be an idiot." Some of these messages are gendered, like "man up" and "don't be a little bitch." These messages can come from parents, relatives, teachers, friends, and classmates, among others. Most of us have come to believe that harsh words and punishment are the best way to cope with difficult situations and feelings. Sometimes it seems like our whole society—from parents and coaches to police and the military—gives the message that we need to be harsher with ourselves to reach our potential. And that the vulnerable, scared, angry, or sad parts of us should be punished and sent away. Feminist author Geneen Roth (1998) summed this up when she discussed many people's relationships with their bodies, weight, and food: "For some reason, we are truly convinced that if we criticize ourselves, the criticism will lead to change. If we are harsh, we believe we will end up being kind. If we shame ourselves, we believe we will end up loving ourselves. It has never been true, not for a moment, that shame leads to love. Only love leads to love."

We internalize these messages and begin to think these harsh thoughts about ourselves. Sometimes we even wish that parts of ourselves would go away, or that those parts are stupid, childish, or ugly. That leaves us with shame, loneliness, and depression as we believe more and more the myths that our culture teaches us about how we're supposed to look and act.

In fact, it's very common for TGD people to have negative thoughts and feelings when they see themselves in the mirror or hear their voices recorded.

One of the youths, Louis, whom you will meet again in the next chapter, described hating his body and experiencing a lot of dysphoria, plus harsh thoughts about his size, but he realized that pushing away parts of himself because other people criticize and judge them only caused more pain and less resilience. This realization began his journey of finding self-compassion. Dropping criticism and learning to love his body helped him find his way to a happier and healthier relationship with himself.

So then, what is self-compassion when you're TGD? In part, it can start by recognizing those thoughts you think about yourself as ugly, harmful, and false ideas from the rest of the world, and rejecting those instead. For example, the whole idea of binary gender is from white and Western culture, but social media and other people believe it so much that they act like it's more natural to be a masculine cisgender man, or a feminine cisgender woman. Even what masculine and feminine look like are pretty much made up and change over time and are different in different cultures. So part of self-compassion is identifying what you learned from those around you and then unlearning those messages.

And for TGD people, self-compassion is the other half of being in community. As we mentioned, resilience for all people is much stronger when they have a supportive community. You probably already have people who you care about and support, but the care you give to others is really only half of that equation. You must also be able to receive care from others *and* from yourself. You're part of your community, so when you recognize that your suffering is not so different from many others'—that your pain is part of being human—this really helps develop self-compassion. Here is something you can try: just as you might remind your friend that they're not alone when they have a hard time, when you have a hard time, you can remind yourself of this, too. Self-compassion is treating yourself like a really good friend. And for TGD people, a really good friend reminds you that you look great, are lovable, and are totally worthy of great things!

WHAT SELF-COMPASSION IS NOT

There are a lot of misunderstandings about self-compassion. Some people think that it's just doing nice things for yourself, feeling sorry for yourself, pretending that you're the best at everything, or even treating yourself like a baby. None of these things are true. Self-compassion is much bigger and more powerful than you might think.

Self-Compassion vs. Self-Care

Although self-care and self-compassion are both important, they're different from each other. Self-care can be thought of as the actions you take as a result of the compassion you have for yourself. Self-compassion is the *attitudes* and *thoughts* you have toward yourself. Self-care is made up of the things you do to take care of your mind and body. If you attempt self-care without developing self-compassion, you might end up not really helping yourself that much. After all, what's it like to take care of a person you don't even like that much? Self-care, when you're learning that you really do deserve it, can be very healing.

Self-Compassion vs. Self-Pity

Self-compassion is not self-pity. It's natural to feel sorry for ourselves at times but self-pity is when we go so deeply into "poor me, life is unfair" mode that we never feel the relief of acceptance. Of course, life can be very, very unfair, especially for TGD youth. We're not saying to pretend life is fair when it's not. However, deep self-pity keeps us angry and isolated by preventing us from seeing how so many others are suffering like we are. It keeps us stuck in feeling bitter, victimized, and hopeless. When we're stuck in self-pity, we feel sorry for ourselves as the only person who has ever felt this bad. In this position, most people decide that life is just very unfair to them and try to use anger to get it all to go away. In self-pity, we don't accept ourselves but remain determined to get away from the parts of ourselves that are suffering.

Self-compassion looks more like turning toward the parts of ourselves we don't like and offering them gentleness and acceptance, and then, remembering that we're suffering alongside many others. It means being patient with ourselves in our most painful moments and accepting all that comes with it. Anger can be a normal response, and accepting the anger is important. And the next self-compassionate step is to look to where we also need to acknowledge our sadness, fear, and shame, and the thoughts that we're unworthy, unlovable, or a failure. Those are the thoughts and feelings that need attention and soothing.

Self-Compassion vs. Self-Esteem

Lots of people talk about self-esteem and on the surface, it may sound a lot like self-compassion. After all, self-esteem is regarding yourself highly—as deserving of good things—and can include self-praise and patting yourself on the back. It basically means seeing yourself as good. This is great, and you should absolutely pat yourself on the back when you've done something great! But what happens when you experience moments that aren't that good? We all fail tests sometimes, get broken up with, lose jobs, mess up, get angry with people, and say things that are less than kind. What happens to self-esteem then? Some research even suggests that those with very high self-esteem can be more self-centered or tend to ignore or reject parts of themselves that are less than great (Hyatt et al. 2018; Neff and Vonk 2009). But self-compassion means accepting yourself regardless of your actions. If you say something mean to your friend, self-compassion means taking care of the part of you that was so angry. If you fail a test, self-compassion doesn't care if you're great in that subject or not, it reminds you that you deserve to feel soothed and cared for no matter how you did.

Self-Compassion vs. Becoming a Bad Person

Keep in mind that self-compassion doesn't mean that you don't try to do better. Some people might think that without self-punishment you might never correct your errors or learn to do better. A key part of our culture's legal system depends on the idea that people do better only if they're punished. But if you think about how you would treat a friend who made a serious mistake, you may realize that your support for them might actually help them do better next time.

In our experience, understanding and acceptance are necessary to making a change. And you can provide understanding and acceptance to yourself! For example, if you lost a job for showing up late, forgiving yourself for being late might be the first step toward figuring out why you showed up late in the first place. If you try to fix something without self-compassion, it can easily turn into being cruel, stubborn, or angry with yourself.

Self-Compassion vs. Babying Yourself

Some people think that all this talk of self-forgiveness and acceptance means that having self-compassion would result in treating yourself like a baby. Some people may feel uncomfortable because it seems too gentle in a harsh world. *How would it help*, you might wonder, *to be more gentle and accepting when I need to* actually *survive? People don't survive by being nice.* To a certain extent, this is true. A tough attitude might be needed to stay strong and survive in your world. Dr. Kristin Neff, a psychologist and the author of a number of books on developing self-compassion, differentiates between gentle and fierce self-compassion (Neff 2021). Gentle self-compassion describes the ways that you're more accepting, kind, and encouraging of yourself. Fierce self-compassion is also important. This is the idea that we sometimes need to be tough in order to show ourselves self-respect and self-love and to protect ourselves and others. For example, if you got rejected after applying for a job, one way to be kind to yourself is to remind yourself that everyone gets rejected sometimes, and that you'll apply to jobs in the future and get one. Fierce self-compassion might help you stick up for yourself and your dignity. You might think something like, *Well, I don't even want to be someplace that doesn't want me.* Gentle self-compassion might say, *It's so hard and painful to be bullied. No wonder I feel down, sad, and angry.* Fierce self-compassion might say, *I would never treat another human that way and whatever they do, I'm not letting them get me down. I need to think of some other ways to respond so I can put a stop to this.* We think that a combination of gentle and fierce self-compassion can keep you resilient even if you need to have a tough exterior. Dr. Neff (2011) reminds us that studies show that people with more self-compassion are often able to feel more empowered and braver to deal with tough situations.

DEVELOPING SELF-COMPASSION

Although there are many approaches to developing self-compassion, these basic steps are the ones we have found really helpful when we practice them regularly. We recommend trying this out and if you find that you like it, try doing it every day for a week or two. You might find that it takes time to notice changes, but eventually you may realize that you're thinking of yourself with more kindness and less harshness.

Before you start, find a quiet place where you can sit comfortably. You may wish to write down a few things or draw pictures, so get out your journal.

Step 1: Stop and notice.

This first step is to practice noticing any harsh or self-critical thoughts and feelings that are coming up. The key here is to simply notice, without trying to change at this point. Let any of these harsh thoughts just come to mind, without trying to push them away or judge them. You might look for thoughts like *I'm a freak*; *If I'm TGD, it means I'm gross*; or *I'm ugly*. A lot of TGD people have harsh feelings of shame, self-hatred, or anger toward themselves. Take a moment and write down labels for these thoughts and feelings like "Being harsh on myself" or "Shame" or "Beating myself up." While you're doing this, be sure you're not trying to push away the thoughts—for now, you're just being curious as if you were a careful, caring detective. You might think about how you would help a friend who, say, fell and hurt their knee. You would look at the bruised knee with curiosity and gentleness, but you would want to have a close look! So have a really close look at these thoughts and feelings, and take some time to draw or write a little about what these are like for you.

A lot of people don't know this, but our emotions are mainly experienced in our body, so see if you can notice how your feelings are experienced. You might need to mentally search around different parts of your body. They might feel sharp or cold or dull or hot. You may notice tightness or burning or numbness. Be sure to check places like your throat, chest, and back. Don't rush this stage. As much as you can, add your body feelings into your writing and drawing. You might have some feelings of dysphoria come up when you experience those feelings in your body. If you can, stay with it and be curious about those feelings too. Do you have mean thoughts about your body? Try to stay gentle and curious with these too.

Step 2: Acknowledge the source of harsh thoughts.

Take a moment to recognize how hard it is to be self-compassionate in a world that is seldom compassionate to TGD people. Those harsh messages about your body, gender, emotions, or behaviors have come from outside you. Babies are not born ashamed of themselves; it is a culture of transphobia that has taught you that how you are is somehow shameful. If you have other marginalized identities (identities that are discriminated against), include those too. Now write out a new message for yourself: "Being compassionate toward myself in a world that teaches harmful myths about [insert your identities here] is so challenging. The messages I've been giving myself come from other people. I can give myself a new message." Truly, it's a radical act to reject these messages.

Step 3: Soothe hard feelings.

Now you have some words and pictures for the harsh thoughts and feelings you have toward yourself. You also have an important reminder that these harsh thoughts and feelings came from other people, based on myths about TGD people and other identities. So this step involves soothing those tough feelings that have been brought up. This, itself, is an act of self-compassion and can be used whenever you're feeling hard on yourself. We start with the body because any parts of your body that are tense, painful, or experiencing other challenging sensations can be soothed. And by soothing your body, these harsh emotions and thoughts can also calm down.

Look at what you wrote or drew about where your body was feeling difficult sensations. Try putting your hands on that part of your body. One way of doing this is to feel in your body for any places that are feeling the emotions, then place your hands on the part of your body that is feeling the harshness the most. If doing this brings up dysphoria, you can try imagining yourself placing your hands on your body, or try locations on your body that bring up less dysphoria. When you place your hands, try to feel their warmth there. Imagine calm, soothing energy going into these painful spots on your body. Just notice what happens. Does the sensation change at all? It might not go away completely, but that's okay. Does the sensation grow? Shrink? Does it change in intensity? Whatever comes up is okay. You may experience other emotions arising, such as sadness or anger. This is okay too. Try to accept whatever happens when you do this part of the exercise without trying to get any of the sensations to go away. To really bring the soothing home, you might draw a picture of the part of your body—say, your arms—being calmer and more soothed. Your author Deb likes to imagine light streaming onto a part that is feeling especially tense or painful. You can draw whatever works for you.

Step 4: Rework your thoughts.

Actively try to find more compassionate ways to think about and treat yourself. In the first step, you may have noticed harsh statements you directed toward yourself. Remind yourself that you think harsh things toward yourself because the world has taught you many myths, such as the idea that by being harsh on yourself, you will do better, or that you're "less than" others because of your identity.

Now, try to find a more compassionate way to talk to yourself. It might help here to think of what you would say if you were talking to a close friend. If they said, "I'm so stupid," you might say, "Hey, you're not stupid. Everyone fails a test sometimes." If they said, "This is all my fault," you might say, "You may have messed up but it's not all your fault. Besides, you were doing your best." So take your self-critical statements and imagine another statement that would be more self-compassionate. Many people find it helpful to write down more compassionate statements. If you like, you can add drawings or illustrations of your new statements.

Here are some examples we have found helpful to say to ourselves:

- I made a mistake but everyone makes mistakes.

- Just like everyone else, I'm not perfect.

- I'm just having a rough time right now. That means I need to be more compassionate toward myself, not less.

- It's not my fault that racism/sexism/homophobia/transphobia exists.

- Like everyone else, I feel sad sometimes.

- I might not look exactly how I want, but I can still be loved and accepted.

- I'm smart about a lot of things.

- This person doesn't love/like me, but I'm basically a good person.

You'll find your own statements. Some keys here are to focus on statements that reflect care, love, forgiveness, and gentleness toward yourself. And to make sure that the statement is something you can believe in. For example, *I'm the greatest person in the world* might sound boosting to your self-esteem, but it's pretty hard to believe for most people. On the other hand, a statement like *Despite my flaws, I'm basically a good person* is pretty believable. You might want to write these in a note on your phone to pull out when you need to remind yourself.

Step 5: Connect.

Research shows that when we connect our tough experiences to the suffering of others, we can be more self-compassionate and more compassionate to others. In the previous step, you probably saw that many of the statements have some part of "like everyone else." This step gets us out of the illusion that we're alone in our pain. Often people are self-critical because they believe in their deepest thoughts that things are all their fault. That is, if you fail a test and you believe it's all your fault, you will be more self-critical than when you remind yourself that people fail tests all the time; it's part of going to school. If you get dumped by your partner, you'll feel much more harshly toward yourself if you believe that you must be a loser.

But when you remind yourself that people get broken up with all the time and those people are also struggling and heartbroken, you might be more gentle with yourself. So, for this step, we'll use an ancient Buddhist technique called *tonglen*, which is designed to increase compassion (Chödrön 2001). In *tonglen*, you connect to the suffering of others to help feel more compassion for yourself and others. So for this step, you might say, *Like so many other people, I am suffering.* And, *Like other people, I also deserve compassion.* Feel free to expand on these statements to make them more specific to you. You might even imagine all the other people in the world who have failed tests, gotten broken up with, experienced discrimination, and so on. Your author Jayme likes to imagine comforting those people and those people comforting them back. Just as we might reassure our friends that they're not alone, here we reassure ourselves that we're not alone. This step may also remind you that you're part of your own community. You probably already think that your friends and the people you love deserve compassion and kindness. This is a moment to remind yourself that just like the people you love, you deserve to show the same compassion to yourself. Imagining yourself showing love to other people who share your identities might be useful. For example, if you're a Latinx nonbinary person, you might imagine other people like you and reminding them that they deserve love and compassion. Try writing down some of these reminders. If you'd like, you can draw the other people who deserve your compassion—and don't forget to add yourself into the crowd!

Step 6: Commit.

For the last step, you're making a commitment to yourself. This step is where you especially might want to bring in some fierce compassion. You might imagine yourself making a fierce commitment to yourself to be kinder and gentler to yourself as an act of resistance. When the world is harsh, you can be tough in showing yourself care. If you would stand up for a friend, here is where you say you would stand up for yourself. This commitment may feel hard at first. After all, if you have been giving yourself messages that you don't deserve self-compassion, it will be hard to commit to it. So, start slow if you need to. Perhaps at first you just say, *I will try to be more self-compassionate* or even, *I will try these exercises again this week*. Include this commitment in your journal.

PRACTICING THESE STEPS

We invite you to do any or all of these steps. If only one works for you, do that one. If you need to change the order or what you say or do, do that. Do what works for you. We do encourage you to try to practice this at times when you find yourself being especially self-critical, and even at times when you don't. Even if you stop for a moment when you're getting frustrated with yourself, and remind yourself that being harsh won't help, that's a positive step. The more you practice, the easier this gets until it's somewhat automatic. Ideally, you'll take a few moments each day to practice this, so it's easier at times when you're being especially self-critical. Practicing will help your body and mind remember that it's possible to soothe hard thoughts, that your harshest thoughts can be reworked, and that you're not alone.

There are many ways you can practice, and the idea is to make these steps your own. One way we recommend is using the series of sentences and drawings you've made already. By going through steps 2–6, you can remind yourself of new images and words to rework difficult thoughts, and by soothing parts of you that are feeling your pain, you also have some ideas and images of sharing and sending compassion to others like you. And lastly, you've made a new commitment to continue forward on your journey. Reviewing this and repeating the soothing, reworking, and compassion-sending steps are available to you any time.

Another way we recommend is to start over with the process any time you wish. We'd suggest that you do this when you feel that the thoughts and feelings you've written or drawn no longer seem as important.

We also encourage you to return to this chapter as you continue on through the book. If the self-care exercises seem too hard, for example, it may be that you need to return to self-compassion. We firmly believe that resilience hinges on increasing self-compassion and treating yourself more like you would treat a close friend. After all, once you're showing self-compassion, you can always be your own source of the most reliable healing and resilience.

In the next chapter, we'll cover making friends with your body. Sounds simple, but taking good care of yourself in a tough world is serious business. Don't worry, we have a lot of tips.

TAKEAWAYS

* Self-compassion might be the most important foundation for anyone wanting to have more resilience, and it's especially important for TGD people living in a world that teaches a lot of ugly myths about being transgender.

* It's easy to swallow transphobic myths and messages and start to treat yourself harshly or blame yourself for what's hard in your life.

* This chapter showed you some techniques that can help you quickly find more ways to be your own good friend. By teaching yourself new messages, you can start to unlearn those myths and mean-spirited, self-critical thoughts. The steps are:

    * Stop and notice.

    * Acknowledge the source of harsh thoughts.

    * Soothe hard feelings.

    * Rework your thoughts.

    * Connect.

    * Commit.

* The radical act of refusing the transphobia that exists in our culture is a really important way to get yourself through tough times and find the community and life you want. After all, who can be a better friend to you, than you?

CHAPTER 3

MAKING FRIENDS WITH YOUR BODY

Throughout our lives, we have a constant companion. It never leaves us, even when we're angry or neglectful. In our hardest moments and our best moments, our body remains with us. It's the source of some of the most amazing pleasure and happiness we feel! And yet, for many TGD people, the body is also a source of frustration, anger, shame, disgust, hopelessness, anxiety, or depression. Why is this? Why do so many TGD people feel distress related to their bodies?

Earlier we talked about gender dysphoria, the distress you feel when you experience your body (including its shape, size, and features, but also things like your voice, your gestures, and other aspects of being in your body) as not corresponding with your gender identity. While that's true for many, it's not the whole picture or even a necessary part of being TGD. First, not all TGD people experience gender dysphoria. In fact, some TGD people experience a lot of pride, joy, and satisfaction in their bodies. Second, for those who do feel this dysphoria, the amount of distress they feel usually changes over time, maybe even day to day or hour to hour.

Some piece of body dissatisfaction can come from the distress of gender dysphoria, but for many, it's a more complex picture. So what's going on? How can we understand the whole picture of what contributes to so many TGD folks feeling distressed and unable to find any sense of satisfaction and pride in their bodies?

There are two major things to look at when you're trying to understand your experience of your body as a TGD person: (1) your internal experience of your body expression being different from what you expect, and (2) your external experience of how others respond to your body expression. Let's say a bit more about these.

When it comes to internal experience, many TGD people experience their bodies as not quite the way they want them to look or feel. Catching sight of yourself in the mirror, needing to shower, or being called the wrong pronoun can bring up painful reminders that your internal experience of your gender doesn't quite match how your body appears. Author and psychotherapist S. J. Langer (2019) proposes that the minds of TGD people may have a "map" of their bodies. And when their mind's map doesn't match their actual body in ways that relate to gender, it creates discomfort: the mind expects a particular gendered body and responds with really uncomfortable feelings when it doesn't find it. This painful experience is what leads many TGD people to seek ways to resolve this. You might have already changed your hair, clothes, or makeup, or even the way you talk or stand to be a better fit for your gender. These are ways that you're already dealing with dysphoria. (If you're experimenting or unsure about your gender or how you want to look, check out some of the many books and guides for TGD youth, including *The Gender Quest Workbook* [2019], another book by your authors.)

These changes may even mean you've experienced *gender euphoria*, or the feeling of joy or contentment when you feel more at home in your body. Some people go on to consider hormones or other interventions to change their bodies. These interventions should be discussed with a doctor, a therapist, or another professional who has expertise in this area. As we said in chapter 1, if you feel that dysphoria is so painful that it's overwhelming you, you might need to seek this help sooner rather than later.

Changing your clothes, hair, how you walk or talk are ways to change the internal sense of gender, and also help ensure that your external experience or your gender expression works better for you by making it more likely that people will respond to you in ways that fit better for how you feel about yourself. A lot of people feel gender euphoria when they finally can wear clothes that fit their gender or find a hairstyle that really suits their identity. Even with this, our culture is not always good at recognizing identities, and for those who are nonbinary, being called "sir" or "miss"—because that's normal in English—can feel pretty bad.

You may very well be thinking about or planning for other, bigger changes, like gender-affirming hormones or surgery. We encourage you to explore all of your options thoroughly with a gender-affirming mental health or medical professional, if you think this is what you want. At http://www .newharbinger.com/54193, you can read about finding reliable, affirming medical information. There's a lot of misinformation out there, and some of it is outright transphobic, so proceed with caution.

And, if you read books or see social media or even news articles about TGD people, you might start to think that once they get hormones and have surgery, all their suffering will be gone. But many TGD people don't want or need these interventions, and even for those who do, there is one more way that our TGD bodies are linked to suffering: through the unnecessary suffering of being judged and discriminated against for how you look or identify.

In this chapter, we will be talking about how messages from our culture about TGD bodies end up causing us pain and harm because of the ways we start to believe them. This part can hurt you even if you have your body looking close to what you want. We'll visit with Louis, a young transgender person, and read his story of learning to love his body. And we'll learn some new techniques to connect with your body in ways that feel good to you, as well as how to use your body as a resource for feeling better and even healing as you discard unwanted social messages.

MESSAGES ABOUT YOUR BODY

Even for those who feel satisfied with how their bodies look, those whose bodies don't fit neatly in the gender boxes of "man" and "woman," or "boy" and "girl" may experience feeling excluded, bullied, harmed, or discriminated against because of their appearance. Other people's ideas about our bodies have a lot of influence on our own thoughts about ourselves; we start to internalize the stigma of these negative messages. You can probably already think of ways that our culture gives you and others messages about what the ideal body looks like. Think of some of the messages you've received about your body. Do you ever repeat them to yourself? How many of these messages do you think come from outside you? Once we identify that an idea has gotten under our skin, we can start to distance ourselves, and have our own, new thoughts.

Cultural ideas that certain body appearances are preferable don't stop at gendered body characteristics. There are many prohibitions in our culture that make looking different from someone who is white, cisgender, thin, and able-bodied really difficult. For those with darker skin, uniquely gendered bodies, visible disabilities, or who are larger, the constant feedback that your body isn't accepted is painful and can cause anxiety, depression, and anger. These feelings can add to the negative and harsh thoughts you have about yourself. It can be so hard to feel accepting and proud of your body when so many messages are telling you not to.

Black therapist and author Resmaa Menakem (2017) said that the trauma of racism—and other traumas—live in and on the body and can only be healed through the body. This is an important reminder that the ways our culture communicates these ugly messages about certain bodies actually hurts us. Stress is not good for our bodies, and all the things people do to cope with stress—like self-harm, eating too much junk food, using drugs or alcohol to numb themselves—also hurt our bodies. If you do any of these things, it's not because you're bad or weak; you may be trying to cope with the stress in the best way you can right now, even if you wish you could be a better friend to yourself by avoiding these things.

BODIES, EMOTIONS, AND COMING HOME

People often use harmful coping behaviors because of how bad they feel due to growing up with negative messages about themselves, plus gender dysphoria. These bad feelings might show up in your body as tension, restlessness, jitteriness, heaviness, nausea, or other unpleasant sensations when you're feeling anxious or sad. Our emotions, good or bad, are experienced in and through our bodies. So when the world has you feeling upset, scared, or out of sync with your body, you're likely also experiencing some unpleasant physical sensations. Stress, trauma, anxiety, and depression can additionally make it difficult to feel anything *but* these unpleasant sensations. In fact, chronic stress and trauma (experiencing severe threats to your well-being that disrupt your ability to feel safe in the world) can make your body get "stuck" in fear and tension. Even beyond the feeling of gender dysphoria, other life experiences can contribute to feeling at odds with and uncomfortable with your body.

You might wonder, in light of all of this, *How* could *I also feel at home in my body?* Seems like home is a pretty difficult place to be for a lot of people.

While it can be hard for you to find peace, satisfaction, and pride in your body, it's far from impossible. So many people just like you are on this journey to reclaiming joy and freedom in their bodies. Even when there are things they wish to, or plan to, change about their bodies, many people have found ways to greater calm, strength, and contentment in and through their bodies. We believe you can, too. Resmaa Menakem (2017) reminds us: "Years as a healer and trauma therapist have taught me that trauma isn't destiny. The body, not the thinking brain, is where we experience most of our pain, pleasure, and joy, and where we process most of what happens to us. It's also where we do most of our healing, including our emotional and psychological healing. And it's where we experience resilience and a sense of flow."

To help us really understand what it's like to start to love your body, we spoke with Louis. Louis is sixteen and has been through a lot to come to terms with his identity. He was not only figuring out how to love his trans body, but also his brown skin and what he calls his "chubby" body. Most of the time, TGD people are also navigating other identities and aspects of their bodies that they have been taught are not good, not attractive, or less valuable than other people's. Louis first described his experience of being bigger bodied in a world that values thinness and went on to share how he learned to be more comfortable with his body.

⁺★ LOUIS'S STORY: Learning to Love the Mirror

I'm gonna start with my chubby body, being overweight and whatnot. At first, I was very ashamed and self-conscious. I wore bigger clothes, both for dysphoria and because I was chubby. Over time, I realized I know myself, and I know I don't have the motivation to work out, to change the shape of my body. And if that's not gonna change, something has to. And I realized it's gonna have to be the way I think about my body and the way I see it.

The first thing I started doing was actually seeing it, looking at it, and making myself look at myself so I could know what I looked like. Because you can't really love yourself if you don't know what you look like, you know? I began slowly introducing myself to my body. I actually used Snapchat, where you can take pictures and only you can see them. So I started just taking pictures of me in my binder so I could get used to what my stomach looks like, what I look like. At first it was like a chore but after a while, I started enjoying it. It made me happy. You can even see in the photos that at first I'm frowning and over time I start smiling. Sometimes I'd record myself singing, and I just started having a good time with it. After a while, I began to feel more comfortable and more like myself in my body. And after a while, I began to like it and I began to enjoy it more and more. So now I'm at a point where I feel happy wearing more revealing clothing, like I got a little tank top that

I would've never worn a year ago. Now I like wearing it and I feel a lot more happy.

Louis then described his struggle to make friends with his body as a TGD person. The pain he experienced, especially related to chest dysphoria, was devastating and got in the way of his being able to enjoy his life. He described how he survived the wait between knowing he wanted top surgery at age thirteen to when he was able to get surgery at age sixteen:

My gendered body is going to be hard to talk about because of how painful the dysphoria was. I kinda just blocked out a lot it. For me, at first it was kinda just about survival, you know, wearing baggy clothes, wearing my brother's old clothes, just anything I could do to feel more comfortable, and there was no room for self-expression. It was just whatever I could do to feel less awful. And then over time as I got access to things like binders and gender therapy and whatnot, it became less about survival, and there became more and more room to express myself, to do fun things like paint my nails and eventually dye my hair, get a buzz cut when I wanted to. Once I began to accept that this was my reality, that I would have to wear binders for a while, that I probably would wear baggy hoodies, even in the summer, once I began to adjust to that, I made room to have fun with it. To do little things to make it better. Now that I'm post top surgery, a lot of that survivalness about it is gone. It's like I made it through the worst of it and now I can express myself in fun ways. It was definitely a rough journey, but I made it through and I'm a lot happier and I can have a lot more fun with how I present myself.

This is the story for a lot of TGD folks. The process of learning to first see and then accept and finally love your body can be a long one! This can make it hard to feel whole and to find your own best way. There can be great power, though, in reclaiming your body from these messages, from past harm, finding out what is true for you, and moving toward acceptance, pride, and peace. Basically, we're talking about finding more and more ways to make your body your home—even at the same time you're considering the ways you want to change your body.

Think of your body as a house that is yours forever. You probably don't love everything about your "house," so there may be things you might change, like adding another room, renovating the kitchen, or removing a wall. Like Louis, you might really need to make some changes in order to relieve your dysphoria. Those are big projects that will take time. But there are other things you can do, like changing furniture, curtains, or paint that can make you feel a bit more comfortable in your home while you make plans for these big changes. And meanwhile, you can learn to love the whole house. This means finding what you like about your house. Maybe other people say it's too big or too small. You can say, "It's the house I have and I'm going to love it because it's where I live." People might say, "Oh without this extra room, you don't have a real home." Well, every home is different and the thing that makes it a home is that *you* live there.

Finding ways to love your home, even while you plan to make renovations, makes sense—you'll be living with most of that house for your whole life, regardless of what others think or say. So, remember, your liberation from ugly messages lies in your ability to find a way to be at home in your body even if you look forward to some "renovations."

As a multiracial person, Louis had an additional obstacle to coming home to his body: he struggled to feel good about his brown skin, especially because nearly everyone else in his school was white. He described how he became prouder of his skin, only to be thrown a curveball when he learned that not everyone saw him as a person of color.

✦ LOUIS'S STORY: Discrimination, Confusion, and Dysphoria

My racial ambiguity has been a very up-and-down journey, where like with my body positivity, there were little ups and downs, but overall it was an upward progression. With my race, it has really been up and down. At first I hated that I didn't look like the people around me. I hated that I felt worse than them, I felt gross, I felt that they wouldn't see me the same, that I wasn't a person in the same way that they were. I had to be more like a better person, I had to be nicer and kinder and more fun and more intelligent, to be given the same respect as them.

Because I thought something was inherently wrong with me, something about me would make them uncomfortable, I spent a long time feeling and thinking that I had to make up for it. I don't know what made me want to change that, but I did, and over time I began to enjoy my brownness. I began to realize that was something that made me different, and not in a bad way. And after a while, I felt proud. I felt proud to be different, I felt proud to have a different experience than my white peers, and I enjoyed it. And then I was told that I look white by someone, and that made me realize that this isn't as black and white as me being white or me being brown. And that kind of set me back. If I'm proud of being brown, and then I'm told that I'm not brown, where am I now? And now I'm more in a place of accepting that I'm maybe both, maybe neither. I don't think I'll ever get a set label on that because if I come up with one, everyone around me is gonna have a different label. They're gonna see me differently. And the way they'll interact with me is different from person to person. So right now I think I've accepted that I'll never have a set answer. I'll just have to accept that it's going to be ambiguous, and I think over time I'm growing more comfortable with being something in between.

In Louis's story, we see the reality of discrimination, confusion, and dysphoria, how hard it is to live with these things and the impact on the relationship to your body. We also see Louis reclaiming their right for their body to be a source of pride, pleasure, fun, resilience, and resistance. Louis found a way to be "home." But how do you get from one to the other? You might start by finding some ways, even small ones, to be better "friends" with your body. Taking your body back might be hard and take time, but in the end, your body is yours. Will you choose to get fierce about defending what's yours?

After all, no matter what, our bodies are always doing their best to protect us and function well, even when they're not able to do the best job at it. And our bodies are also such an important source of information about our emotions: they're the best way we experience joy and pleasure. But it can be tough to experience the pleasure of good food, a hug, holding a pet, or noticing the new spring flowers when our bodies feel out of sync, shameful, or frightening to live in. Adding experiences of trauma to the mix makes it hard to connect to your body at all. Yet, those pleasurable experiences are some of the main ways that we, as humans, have to feel at peace and at home.

CONNECTING TO YOUR BODY

In the rest of this chapter, we're going to give you things you can do to go from distress to acceptance, satisfaction, and even pride. If there are things you want to change about your body, including gender-affirming interventions, you may find that improving your connection to your body helps you reduce stress and anxiety as you go through those processes.

The hardest part is just believing it's possible to change your relationship with your body. You might be thinking, *Why would I want to make friends with a body that causes me so much stress? How do I even connect with my body through trauma?* Or, *I'm going to need gender-affirming interventions to feel like connecting.* These are legitimate thoughts and, in the end, you may still have stress, trauma, and dysphoria. However, as Louis explained, these things can be easier to deal with and heal when you come from a place of greater connection with yourself. This is because when you're connected with yourself, you treat yourself as a friend. And just as you would still stand up for, accept, and defend an imperfect friend, you can learn to stand up for, accept, and defend yourself, instead of beating yourself up with more pain and self-hatred. You have to become a fierce defender of yourself, instead of a fierce attacker of yourself. When you're a better friend to yourself, you'll stop giving yourself mean messages that add more pain and stress. This is why we talk about making friends with your body.

Even though one of the most important ways you can feel stronger and more confident is to make friends with your body, that friendship doesn't need to be perfect. Once we start to form a friendship with our bodies, even an uneasy one, we can begin to take our place in the world despite the world's messages. When we start to fiercely reclaim our bodies from trauma and negative messages, we can sometimes find that extra confidence in the face of tough times. We can be clearer about what changes we do and don't need. We can stand up for ourselves with others, and we can find ways to experience pleasure and joy along the way. Plus, in a crisis, those who have found even a little acceptance of their bodies have more resources to turn to: confidence and clarity in their bodies. Our bodies are so important for helping us find grounding, calm, and even the capacity for pleasure. But to get access to these, we need to gently reconnect to our bodies with some compassion and acceptance.

We encourage you to approach our suggestions and exercises with a lot of gentleness and slowness. Return to the chapter on self-compassion when you find yourself encountering shame or overwhelming negative feelings about your body. Improving your relationship with your body might take time and may sometimes feel like an up-and-down journey, and that's okay. Be patient and compassionate with yourself, knowing that you're tackling something really big and important here. If you experience dysphoria, trauma, or pain in your body to the extent that anything here makes it much worse, we strongly suggest that you stop, slow down, and go back to using any of the suggestions or exercises that have helped. If you experience severe trauma or dysphoria in your body in ways that are causing you a great deal of suffering, we suggest that you also work with a TGD-affirming mental health professional. And, as always, if you start to feel so bad that you think about wanting to end your life, it's time to contact a hotline such as The Trevor Project or the Trans Lifeline right away so you can get support from people who understand.

You may have had meditation, mindfulness, yoga, or other similar practices recommended to you. While we find these to be powerful practices in our own lives, they can be tough for anyone struggling with accepting themselves and their body, with trauma, or with past negative religious or spiritual experiences. The practices we recommend here are designed especially to be gentle and helpful for people feeling uneasy about their bodies.

Remember too that these are *not* things you first try in a crisis; they're *practices* of getting to know yourself. This means they require repetition and slow exploration and progression. Choose a few you like and practice a few times a day. Just like you would not turn to a stranger for support when you go through a horrible breakup, you should make friends with your body over time, so it's there for you when you need it. Remember to be patient and compassionate with yourself as you explore.

Likewise, these are not practices meant to eliminate gender dysphoria. While some people may find it easier to cope with gender dysphoria as a result of these suggestions, our hope is that you can simply feel more friendly with your body, and more able to quiet negative internal messages about your body. You may still want or need changes to your body in order to feel comfortable. We support all the pathways that TGD people follow to find more comfort, more happiness, more satisfaction, and more gender content-ment or euphoria.

Pleasant Sensations

One simple place to start is by learning to experience pleasant sensa-tions in your body. Many people with dysphoria or depression, or who have experienced trauma, lose their ability to experience pleasant sensations. Try things like holding a soft blanket, stroking a pet, holding a smooth stone, or running your hands under warm water. You can also try using other senses to experience pleasant sensations, like finding a nice smell, listening to the rain, or looking at clouds. Experiment! Move your focus into the sensation, and try to let yourself experience it without judgment. Then, try to slow down your breathing and see if you can let the good feeling spread at all, or if it just stays with your hands (or ears, nose, tongue, or eyes). Savor each pleasant sensation. See if you can notice every part of the sensation. What changes? What stays the same? What feels really good? You may notice that while trying these things, your emotions shift and soften.

Try practicing this a few times a day—maybe while you're walking or as you fall asleep at night. You can do this anywhere. Reminding yourself that your body can experience pleasant sensations is one way you can reteach your body that, although you have negative sensations, you also have posi-tive ones.

Finding a Calm or Neutral Place in Your Body

As we've said, our bodies are the main way we experience our emotions. If a lot of your emotions are unpleasant, you will also have difficult feelings in your body, like tension, restlessness, headaches, feelings of squeezing or pain. But at the same time, it's possible to shift and change those sensations, thereby changing your emotions.

Practicing finding neutral, calm places in our body when we feel okay can help us use those places as a resource when we're upset. Take a few moments when you feel at ease to try to mentally scan your body for any places that already feel comfortable or even good just on their own. Usually, people find it hard to pay attention to those places because the tension and distress are much "louder" in their bodies, so be sure to consider some areas that you don't usually think of. Many people feel neutral in their upper arms, for example, but you should find your own calm places. Undoubtedly, you will find areas that are very uncomfortable, in pain, numb, or having other discomfort. You can note those with a lot of kindness—your author Jayme likes to say "I see you" or "I hear you" to those spots—and move on to find more neutral zones. Once you find them, try placing your hands (if possible) and your attention in that area. Notice any feelings or sensations that arise. Just be with this body part for a while. You don't need to do anything. Just notice what it's like. You might try this several times a day to start to making friends with those parts and to increase your experiences of knowing what it's like to feel pleasant, easy sensations. This doesn't mean that painful, uncomfortable parts are gone—just that you don't ignore the calm places.

Moving Pleasant Sensations

The next step to reteaching your body to access calm, pleasant sensations is expanding the good sensations and helping them be a good resource for places that are uncomfortable. For example, once you've had some good practice noticing pleasant or neutral areas of your body, you can try this next step.

First, find that pleasant or neutral part and place your hands on it, just as you did earlier. Take time to calm your breath and really notice the part that is at ease. Next, try moving your hands to a place where you feel more tension or distress. Give yourself a few moments there, and try to soften your experience of the discomfort. Imagine how you might be with a small child who was feeling this discomfort. You might find it helpful to gently press or massage that area. When you're ready, move your hands back to the pleasant area. What do you notice? Try to stay curious. When it feels possible, put one hand on the comfortable area, and one hand on the uncomfortable area to feel both the tense or uncomfortable parts and the neutral or pleasant parts at the same time. What happens? Imagine using the comfort from one area to soften the other. You're reminding your body that even though the distress is loud, the other, pleasant sensations are still available to you. With this reminder, often your mind will follow along and feel more calm. After you've done this practice repeatedly, you may notice that in times of crisis you can more easily turn to your safe havens of calm in your body.

Experiencing Deep Relaxation

Bodies under a lot of stress or that have experienced trauma can get stuck in a lot of tension, which leads to emotional distress. For many people, their bodies are stuck in tense mode and they forget about the "untensing" that should eventually follow. This can happen for many reasons; for example, chronic stress, pain, fear, shame, or trauma can all lock your body into forgetting what it's like to relax deeply.

This next practice can help the places in your body that hold fear, trauma, and tension relearn how to be calm when you're safe. It's been shown that just by suggesting relaxation to our bodies, those parts become more relaxed and feel more pleasant (Stetter and Kupper 2002). You can learn to gently reteach your body, which, in turn, relaxes your mind and emotions.

The way to remind your body is simple: Find a comfortable position where you can be quiet for some time. We recommend lying on the floor or even the ground outside to really feel the support of the surface beneath you. Slow down your breath. When you're ready, say out loud or in your mind, "My arms are warm and relaxed." Repeat these words a few times, then move on to other body parts—especially those that feel tense. You can always go through any body parts that seem to want more relaxation and try to send warmth and relaxation into those parts. You can also imagine those parts being gently warmed by the sun. Don't forget your face—ours are always tensed up in some way! Mix in some other statements like "My breath is calm and easy" or "My heart is calm and steady." If you can think of statements that seem to promote a feeling of safety and wellness in your body, try those too. You might encounter parts of your body that bring up too much dysphoria, trauma, or anxiety to focus on. This is okay and normal. Just send those parts a nice, comforting thought and move on. You can check in with them later if you want.

Deep relaxation takes practice, and it may feel odd at first. With practice, you might find that your body gets better at "untensing" or at least, relaxation doesn't feel quite as weird. Over time you may find that your body gets stronger at returning to a relaxed state. Difficult moments don't need to get stuck in our bodies as much once we remember how to return to rest.

Tapping

Tapping is another way that you can remind your body what being basically okay feels like. Many people find that tapping on their body produces a feeling of calm or relaxation. Try tapping with your fingers on different areas, with an attitude of care and curiosity. Calm your breath and try slowing down, speeding up, with a lighter tap or firmer tap. Notice the sensation of tapping and how your body responds. If this works for you, you might try it a few times a day. You can tap tense or uncomfortable parts any time to remind them that it's okay to be at ease. If you really find tapping helpful, you can look more into the emotional freedom techniques, which use specific patterns of tapping that have been shown to help with stress and anxiety (Clond 2016). At http://www.newharbinger.com/54193, you'll find a link to a full guide on using emotional freedom techniques at home.

Joyful Movement

A common recommendation for people who are feeling unease in their body or experiencing depression or anxiety is to exercise or to go on walks. Research has shown time and time again that exercise is a great way to improve your mental health. If you already enjoy exercise or engaging in sports, that's great! However, movement can bring up a lot of dysphoria for TGD people. You may or may not feel that way. Those who were shamed about their bodies or rejected from sports may have other feelings arise that keep them from exercising.

Rather than thinking about trying to exercise, try thinking of it as engaging in joyful movement. If you're not ready for this, that's okay. Return to the earlier exercises to continue trying to make friends with some parts of your body. When you feel like you're on better terms, you might try joyful movement to see how it feels.

Joyful movement is simply expanding your thinking about movement into whatever movement feels good, creative, or satisfying to you and doing those things for the pleasure of it. Maybe dancing to music you love is really fun for you. Some people get a lot out of gentle contemplative practices like tai chi or restorative yoga. Try several different things to see what feels like a fit for you. If you have been feeling too down or dysphoric to move much at all, start small and keep it fun.

FINDING YOUR MOVEMENT FIT

It's unfortunate that we have been bombarded with messages about exercise and movement that have made moving seem out of reach. And it's unfortunate that so much movement gets overly gendered. If you want to try a class in person, look for language that makes you feel welcome. Many classes now describe themselves as "All bodies welcome," or are advertised as run by queer or TGD people. Look for classes that are about stretching or gentle movement if you're worried that you aren't "athletic" enough. If you don't feel comfortable trying out movement with others, look online for videos.

Watch for messages that pressure you to go harder than you want or are too gendered for your liking. Move on to another if anything like this bothers you. Try searching for other descriptions that might fit, like "stretching for large bodies" or "wheelchair yoga" or "black transgender workout." Thanks to social media, there are literally hundreds of videos out there for TGD people of all bodies, colors, and abilities. You'll find a few of our favorites at http://www.newharbinger.com/54193.

Try sticking to the rule that any movement is good movement. In fact, write that in your journal! That is, if today you only walked up your block, give yourself a reward. The reward might be watching a TV show, playing a video game, having a favorite snack, or asking a friend to tell you what a good job you did. At first you may find that you need to add rewards, such as *always* being sure you have a positive activity after each time you move. You may find that after a bit, the movement becomes its own reward, but if you find yourself dreading any movement, simple rewards can help you get going. Try to take time after you do any movement to note what feels good in your body. Do you feel pleasantly relaxed? At all proud of yourself? Find our worksheets Tracking Your Movement Satisfaction and Your Expectations vs. Your Experience at http://www.newharbinger.com/54193 for samples of how you can add this to your movement practice.

If you really struggle with motivation, you might write down in your journal how horrible you think moving will be before you start, and then write down what it was really like. Usually taking a walk around the block sounds impossible until you step out the door and find that it's not as bad as you thought. When in doubt, try the first step. At http://www.newharbin ger.com/54193, you can download an online worksheet for that, too: Planning for Rewarding Movement Worksheet.

Many TGD people report that movement can increase dysphoria. To reduce dysphoria, you might wear things that increase feelings of gender euphoria (or at least feeling more neutral). Binding your chest, wearing a breast-enhancing bra, and tucking or packing (which some people do to make their crotches look more gender congruent) may all help you feel the right kind of body feedback as you move. On the other hand, some may experience more gender euphoria with specific kinds of movement. For example, those who wish to experience more masculinity in their bodies may find weightlifting to be particularly satisfying. Dance and yoga have given others a sense of grace in their movement. Many TGD people find more confidence, friendship, and connection with their bodies through movement. So experiment—if one type isn't working for you, try another!

EXPANDING YOUR SENSE OF SAFETY

Throughout these exercises, you may have noticed that your body can be a tough place to be, but when you feel safe in your body, it's easier to deal with challenges. Some of the exercises may have helped you find safer places within your body, which is especially important if your body is stuck in a state of fearfulness and anxiety. The next exercises help you expand on those feelings of safety in your body and help make your body more of a refuge, even if you wish it were different. This way, even when you feel uneasy about your body, it can be a help to you when you're having a rough time.

Visualizing a Comforting Place

One way to try to expand a sense of peace and safety in your body is through visualization of a place that is comforting for you. Visualization is an important part of some psychotherapy approaches and can help you develop an internal resource you can draw on whenever you need it. For some people, visualization is hard. For others, the idea of being in a safe place seems impossible. If this is the case for you, we encourage you to think of this place as a peaceful space or even your special space. Like any exercise, it's perfectly okay to skip this exercise if it just feels upsetting or hard. But also keep in mind that you can make the visualization literally whatever you want. Jayme likes to visualize being in a sunny, sweet-smelling field where deer and foxes rest. As always, you can start small and experiment.

To begin, find a quiet place when you have some time to stop and relax. You might do one of the previous exercises, such as tapping or pleasant sensations to become more present and calm. With your eyes open or closed, (most people find closed eyes to be helpful), allow yourself to imagine being in a safe, comforting, peaceful place. It may be indoors or outdoors, imaginary or a place you've been to before. Just let whatever arises, arise. To enhance this safe space, add more details about what it really feels like to be there. Imagine yourself, your clothes, your hair, and your body exactly as they are when you feel most at ease. Imagine your body being relaxed, quiet, and comfortable. Are you indoors or outdoors? If anything at all seems frightening or threatening in this space, gently imagine something else to keep you safe. Jayme visualizes a magical, clear bubble that keeps any insects or crawly things away when imagining the sunny field that is their comforting place. Then visualize people or beings, real or imagined, who truly care about you. You can imagine them around you, protecting you, and sending you love. You might try picturing them reminding you that your body is good, that you're good, and that they're there for you. There are many videos of guided imagery about developing a safe place. You might check them out or record your own to listen to. We recommend doing this exercise daily to develop this inner resource. Over time, whenever you need to find a sense of safety, you can reach out in your mind to this spot and remember what it's like to feel at peace.

Developing Gratitude

Another simple place to start to build acceptance and friendship with your body is a gratitude practice. When you think about it, it's a bit of a miracle that all this heart beating, breathing, digesting, and so forth happens without you even needing to think about it! You might take the time each morning or evening (or both) to write down a simple statement of gratitude about your body in your journal; you can also use your phone to record or type your statement. Even if there are things you aren't content with about your body, try to find one or two things that you can appreciate. Make it specific and make sure you really believe it, such as: "Today I'm grateful to my eyes so I could see my friend" or "Today I'm grateful to my hands so I could play my video game." Or, "Today I'm grateful for my nose so I could smell coffee." Pair this with the pleasurable sensations exercise for a powerful combination. For example, let's say you pick up a smooth stone or shell. You can focus on the pleasant sensation and then write a note of gratitude for your body's ability to experience this. You can also just try setting a reminder on your phone for a specific time of day. When the reminder goes off, stop and find one thing your body is doing for you at that moment. It can be great to review past gratitude notes when you're feeling a lot of dysphoria or just feeling bad about yourself.

Changing Thoughts

If you have been practicing gratitude for a while, you might be ready to think of how to change judgments about your body. Remember, many of these shameful messages are those that we learned somewhere else. None of us were born feeling ashamed of our size or skin color.

Because we get so many outside messages about how bodies should look and work, it can be hard to get those messages out from under our skin. If you live with a disability, you may have even more complex feelings about the ways your body does and doesn't work the way you wish it would.

However, most of us are quick to reassure our friends that they look great and help affirm them in their gender and bodies in all the ways their bodies show up right now, not in some future time. Think of a few friends, and we bet they have mentioned that they hate something about how their body looks or feels. Think of how you feel toward them when they say these things. You've probably told them that they look great!

What would it feel like to say these things to yourself? This doesn't mean that there aren't still ways you experience grief, sadness, or frustration about your body. This is to find out what ugly messages about your body have gotten under your skin and changing them to something more accurate to you.

You might try writing out a few ways you would respond to a friend when they say what they dislike about themselves; choose responses that are true for you. It may feel awkward, untrue, or even really sad to say to yourself, *My body is a good body* or *Like many people's bodies, mine has flaws, and doesn't always feel good to me, and it's still a good body*. Many TGD youth wish to make changes to their body, which can make it hard to find a statement that feels true. Remember, even if you increase acceptance of your body overall, that doesn't mean you can't make some changes in the future. This is about dropping self-criticism and self-hatred. If you can hang out with how odd it feels and try it, you might find a way to believe some statements of kindness to your body, just as you would believe them about a friend. Spend some time trying to come up with something that feels real and true but drops the extra criticism and self-doubt. Write these statements in your journal so you can go back to them. Here are a few to try when you catch yourself falling into thoughts and feelings of shame and criticism about your body. Once you're ready, start writing your own.

- My brown skin is beautiful.

- Like all people, my gender expression is unique to me, and I am proud of mine.

- Although there are parts of my body I need to change, I appreciate many other things about my body.

- People come in all different sizes. I am learning to love my whole body.

- I look great today.

- I'm getting stronger every day.

- I can't change my body in all the ways I want to, but I can find ways to feel more comfortable.

- My body doesn't always work the way I wish it would, but I'm grateful that I have a lovely singing voice.

- I wish my chest were flat/I wish I had breasts, but I love the color of my eyes.

- My legs feel strong today.

When in doubt, you can remind yourself that your body is doing the best it can—flaws, pain, trauma, and all—to support you and your life. Even though your body may not always feel like it expresses your gender in accurate ways, it has the potential to express so many parts of you. For example, what do your clothes say about who you are on the inside? What about your hairstyle, hair color, jewelry, makeup, nails, piercings, and shoes?

What does how you move, how you talk, and how you experience the world say about your culture, what you love, what you're good at, or where you live? All of these things can be important sources of pride in who you are as a whole person, not just a gender.

Try to start catching thoughts during the day that seem to be filled with self-criticism or self-hatred. In those moments, try to replace that thought with something more true for you. If you find that impossible, try to distract yourself with another activity or thought so the critical thought doesn't "hook" you as much. If you find you're overwhelmed with these thoughts, you can change them, or if they're causing you a lot of suffering, you may benefit from finding a TGD-affirmative therapist who can help you move toward greater acceptance.

PRIDE

A lot of what we're proud of can be expressed through our body. And there's a good reason why we call LGBTQ+ celebrations and marches "Pride." In fact, a lot of research shows that for TGD people, pride in community and pride in all of their intersecting identities, such as race, culture, and more, actually helps them feel stronger and more whole (Goffnett and Paceley 2020). Your body can be part of finding all of these parts of pride.

As we read in Louis's story, finding pride in your body is not only possible but can also help you be on the same side as your body. Think about it. When our friends mess up, do things we think are dumb, or even look really ridiculous sometimes, we still stay proud of them. Why should it be different for our bodies? Even if you want to change some things about your body, finding some pride in yourself can help you on that journey to greater contentment with your body. Regardless of what you've been through, your body has been there with you, breathing, thinking, trying. You have stayed alive. And a lot of the pain and suffering about our bodies is hard enough but is made much harder by the oppression of racism, sexism, homophobia, ableism, transphobia, and more. Ask yourself: will you work to free yourself and your body from the added suffering that these oppressions create? In this way, with a sense of pride in the ways you have stayed alive and kept trying, perhaps you can think of your body as the best resource you have to continue to find your own liberation.

We encourage you to continue to try the exercises from this chapter, and if any one of them fits for you, try to do it daily or even more often. These practices take time. Just like it took your whole life to learn negative messages about your body, it will take some time to unlearn those messages. If you find you're struggling with them, that's okay. You can come back later. But as much as you can, keep returning to the practices of self-compassion, self-care (which you'll read about in next chapter), and connecting to your body. These are the building blocks for getting through the toughest times, finding community, and making yourself a life you want to live. Next up, we'll look at some practical skills for making it through moments when you're feeling especially bad—because part of resilience is getting through to better times.

TAKEAWAYS

★ Negative external messages from our culture about how bodies "should" be can lead to pain, self-hatred, and sadness for TGD people.

★ TGD people are already likely to feel gender dysphoria, or like their body is not a good match for their gender.

★ Louis's story helped us see how one young person came to be better friends with his body through fiercely loving himself the way he is.

★ Through a variety of exercises, you can connect to your body and also expand your sense of safety in and around your body.

CHAPTER 4

RADICAL SELF-CARE: STAYING ALIVE AND STRONG

Life is difficult. And life can be tough for people who are facing discrimination and mistreatment because of who they are. Audre Lorde, a Black queer feminist who was a prominent writer and activist in the civil rights movements of the 1960s and 1970s, wrote: "Caring for myself is not self-indulgence, it's self-preservation, and that is an act of political warfare" (1988). When systems of oppression are doing their best to keep you down, self-care becomes even more important as a way to fight these systems. As trans people have increasingly become the target of conservative political agendas, such as restricting affirmative medical care for TGD youth, they constantly get assaulted with messages of not being valuable, worthy, or legitimate. To value yourself and take care of yourself can act as resistance against these harmful messages.

Many people use the term "self-care" to describe extravagant or expensive activities, such as going on vacation or going to a spa. While those experiences could be used as self-care (only on very special occasions for most of us), self-care actually refers to the day-to-day-things we do to stay mentally, emotionally, and physically healthy. It's about tuning into your needs and meeting those needs. This might mean making a regular effort to eat nutritious foods, getting outside every day, making time for friends, maintaining a regular sleep schedule, engaging in fun activities, and so on. Caring for yourself on a daily basis is important, and it's what keeps us healthy enough to deal with the stressors that arise in our typical days.

You'll find that on tougher days, you will need to increase your self-care to feel okay, just as you might need to eat more when you're getting a lot of exercise. Keeping some regular self-care habits going will make it possible for you to increase them when the going gets tough.

Having a solid sense of what you need for self-care and a commitment to doing those things can help make the many stressors of life more manageable as you find new ways to bounce forward. If we're strong and healthy, it can make it easier to survive feelings of dysphoria, depression, and anxiety, or to get through tough situations of not being affirmed for our identity or of being mistreated. If we can keep our tank full, then we're not scraping at the bottom every time something difficult happens.

BUILDING YOUR SELF-CARE ROUTINE

Self-care is not selfish. You may find it difficult to set aside time for yourself, especially if you're a person who often takes care of others, but self-care is something that everyone deserves. When we keep ourselves healthy, it's better for our friends and loved ones, too, because we have filled our own tank so we have energy to be there for others.

You can be flexible and creative about what you decide is self-care. What feels like self-care for one person may not feel like it for another person. For example, you may use exercise as self-care, but another person may experience dysphoria when they exercise, so that wouldn't feel like self-care. That is totally okay—your self-care is *your* self-care. That's the point! It's not for anyone else.

You may also find that what you need for self-care varies from day to day or in different situations. For example, you may find that your mood is better when you eat healthy foods, but when you have a really hard day, ice cream is what you need. Thinking about your self-care should not be taken as an opportunity to beat yourself up for not doing enough...that's *not* self-care! Approach yourself with compassion, and recognize the strengths you already have in your self-care routine. And remember to be self-compassionate—when you find areas where you can get better at taking care of yourself, be kind and gentle with yourself.

One way to get started is by keeping track of how much distress you're feeling over a day. Throughout the day, ask yourself how you're doing. We recommend an easy scale like this: "On a scale of 1 to 10, how stressed do I feel?" One represents no stress; you're feeling pretty great. Three is sort of normal stress, like you had to rush a little to class or you didn't get quite enough sleep. Five is getting pretty uncomfortable. Seven is a lot—sleep might be off, you're overeating or not eating, you feel pretty awful. Ten is the most stress you can imagine. On this scale, we'd suggest that you increase self-care when you get to five or over. At http://www.newharbinger.com /54193, you can download our Stress Scale, or you can just create a simple area in your journal to keep track every day.

Another important tip is to become familiar with signs that your stress is increasing. Everyone has their own signs. One of the authors, Jayme, gets a little twitch in the corner of their eye. Maybe you start to get grumpy, have trouble paying attention to friends, or start increasing your use of substances. Other signs for many people include having trouble sleeping or sleeping too much; overeating or being unable to eat; feeling anxious, shaky, or like your heart is pounding. Headaches, stomachaches, and feeling sick to your stomach can be common in stress. Some people turn to drinking or drugs when they feel very stressed. When you notice these signs, increase your self-care! And if any of these things are happening in a way that is really interrupting your life, or is getting more dangerous for you, it's time to seek support from a trusted person, such as a counselor, teacher, or parent. See our resources section in the back for emergency numbers if you need them.

SELF-CARE HAS MANY ASPECTS

Many parts of us need self-care. Our bodies need care but so do our emotions, our spiritual lives, our school and friend time. It can be helpful to think about what you're doing to address each of these different areas. You may find that you're doing a lot to care for one part of yourself (for example, your emotional self), and a lot less to care for another part (for example, your physical self). We'll be covering physical, emotional, and spiritual self-care as well as self-care when you're neurodiverse, when you're at school or on social media, and more. We recommend that you take an inventory right now of where you feel like you're already taking good care of yourself. As you read along, notice which areas you'd like to add more self-care to, and what you'd like to do in those areas.

Physical Self-Care

The three big ways to quickly improve your mood involve your body. We know, this is what everyone says, but we have to agree that it's all true: sleep, exercise, and good food can change your life.

Sleep is the first of the big three. Getting enough sleep can completely turn a bad mood around. When you're tired, your emotions get all out of whack, it's harder to recover from a difficult experience, and your learning and focus will be off. Ideally, aim for a regular sleep schedule (going to bed and waking up at about the same time each day), where you're getting at least eight hours of sleep. Experts recommend eight to ten hours of sleep a night for people ages thirteen to eighteen.

Exercise is another of the three big parts of physical self-care. Exercise has been shown to increase feeling good about yourself and your ability to think and learn. It also decreases anxiety, depression, and overall bad moods. For all three of your authors, nothing turns a bad day around faster than getting some movement. For some TGD people who don't feel great about their bodies, exercising can be intimidating or hard. If that's you, we recommend rereading the Joyful Movement section of chapter 3. Remember, all movement is good movement!

Nutrition is the third cornerstone of physical self-care. Obviously, eating nutritious foods feeds your body's health, but good nutrition can also have positive impacts on mental health, often providing a more steady mood and improved ability to focus. We have found that there is a ton of misinformation about nutrition, and it can be hard to find reliable sources. But in general, adding more fruits, vegetables, and whole grains to your diet will help you get the nutrition you need to stay well. Staying hydrated seems like clichéd advice, but drinking enough water throughout the day may help with mood, anxiety, focus, and tiredness (Liska et al. 2019). The Institute of Medicine (2005) recommends that teens get about eight cups (sixty-four ounces) of water (or other nonalcoholic drinks) a day, and that number can go up depending on how large your body is and how active you are. One can of sparkling water is about twelve ounces, so picture about five or six of those.

Medical and Sexual Health

Taking care of your body's medical and sexual health needs is another important piece of self-care, and we know that being trans can sometimes make it hard to do things like seeing a doctor or other health care provider. Sometimes health care providers are not affirming or not knowledgeable about helping TGD youth. It might be helpful to call ahead to ask about the provider's experience with *trans-affirmative care* (medical or mental health treatment that recognizes and validates your gender identity) or ask other people who they have found that they like. We also recommend that you call ahead to clarify your name and pronouns so you're not misgendered or called by the wrong name. If you don't feel comfortable making this kind of call yourself, it could be helpful to talk with someone you trust about concerns or fears you have about going to a medical appointment. If you have a parent who is supportive of your gender, that would be a good place to start. If you don't have a supportive parent, you could talk with another trusted adult who you know to be an ally. You could ask that person to help you strategize about how to minimize dysphoria during these visits, how to advocate for yourself, or even ask them for help by making these calls for you.

Sometimes TGD people feel nervous about asking people to address them by their name and pronouns, or correcting people when they're misgendered or called by the wrong name, especially when those people are medical professionals. They sometimes worry about burdening cisgender people with their needs. If you feel this way, please know that you absolutely deserve to be called by the correct name and pronouns. This is a very basic human courtesy you're asking for. If you're worried about making cisgender people feel uncomfortable in that *one* moment, just think about how uncomfortable it feels for you a lot of the time. Your needs matter and you deserve respect!

Some of you may be considering making changes to your body to affirm your gender. We encourage you to access one of the many guides to exploring these choices and getting reliable, affirming information. Keep in mind that there is a huge amount of misinformation on the internet that is designed to be nonaffirming. At http://www.newharbinger.com/54193, we have listed some books and organizations that we think provide solid, affirming medical information and help for those who are considering these options. Gender-affirming therapists, doctors, and clinics may be useful in determining the right steps for you.

Sexual health care is medical care for your sexuality. It includes getting information about how your reproductive system works, avoiding sexually transmitted infections, and preventing unwanted pregnancy. For many TGD people, it can be uncomfortable to get sexual health care because it means talking about genitals or having them examined, which can bring up a lot of dysphoria. After all, if you're feeling like some of your body parts don't really match your gender identity, the last thing you want to do is have them examined!

You might feel a lot better going to a sexual health care provider who is experienced in working with trans people. One way to find a trans-affirmative provider would be to look at websites of your local LGBTQ+ support organizations. These sites will often post lists of local LGBTQ+-affirmative providers. While it may feel uncomfortable, it may be helpful to tell your provider beforehand about your concerns about dysphoria, for example, when having your genitalia examined, so that you and your provider can try to minimize the stress during the appointment.

We get how hard it can be for TGD teens to get to a clinic or doctor. There are a lot of doctors and health care providers who are working hard to be sure that youth like you can get the care you need—but first you have to be able to get to that care! So, to combat the anxiety, dysphoria, or distress you may experience in getting medical care, look at the strategies for emotional self-care in the next section. They will be really useful in helping you make it to appointments and care for yourself afterward. It's not always easy to untangle all these challenges. but it's so important to care for your body and show it love and respect.

If you're struggling with keeping up with your medical and sexual health care, perhaps it would be helpful to prioritize your body's needs. Ask yourself, *What is most important for me to take care of?* If you're sexually active and could get pregnant, it may be very important to learn how to prevent this. Consider talking with a supportive parent or a trusted adult ally to help you think through these challenges. You, along with your trusted adult, might decide that being overdue for your annual physical is not as important as seeking treatment for a rash that is getting worse, and then you can prioritize getting the rash treated. Once you make it through that appointment, you can then think about getting ready to address your need for a physical.

Emotional Self-Care

Emotional self-care involves tuning into your feelings and caring for your mental health. While everyone has sad days, feels nervous or anxious at times, or gets angry, when our emotions get out of balance, we can spend so much time in tough feelings that they start to take over our life. Eventually this can lead to mental health problems, like depression. Even with all the self-care in the world, some people will experience depression or severe anxiety. However, good self-care can help you get through tough times. Remember, if your emotions are so difficult that you start to think you might hurt yourself, it's time to get outside support right away.

What helps you keep your emotions in balance may look very different for you than for some friends because everyone has a different personality and needs. IRL friends and making art might work great for you, but your friend might find that gaming with online friends and listening to music helps them feel better. One key step to emotional self-care is to think about what helps you feel good about yourself, your life, and your day. A lot of people say that being outside, being with animals, doing art, gaming, dancing, laughing, reading, and lots of other things help them have a good day, even if things were hard.

Take a moment to write down in your journal a list of the activities that help you feel good about yourself, stay in balance, and look forward to the next day. These are the things you might want to make sure you're doing most days, and even more often when you're not feeling so great.

People you love. For most people, spending quality time with loved ones and friends is a very important part of having good emotional health. Most people tell us that being around good friends, family (depending on your family!) or people who affirm their gender really helps them stay happy. We keep bringing this up because connecting with supportive people is one of the key things that TGD youth tell us helps them feel great. Listing the people you rely on in your journal might be a great way to remind yourself who to turn to when you need a lift or a friend when you feel lonely. If you don't have many people on that list, that's okay. We will be talking about how to increase your community of friends later on. Meanwhile, remember to ask the people you love for what you need: that might be as simple as getting boba or asking someone to check in with you after a doctor's appointment. Sometimes the people we love need a little education about what we need. If you have a cisgender friend who wants to support you but is never sure how, give them a little information about what support looks like to you.

Supportive self-talk. Some other strategies for emotional self-care focus more on your inner self. One of these strategies is positive self-talk. As we have discussed throughout this book so far, sometimes we talk to ourselves with an inner voice whose words are mean, critical, or even cruel. These words are usually ugly messages we got from outside ourselves. It may be helpful to identify the mean things your inner critic says to you and ask yourself, *Would I say that to a friend?* The answer is usually *No way!* You deserve to treat yourself with as much kindness as you would a friend, so working on challenging your inner critic is important. One way to start to change those ugly messages is called "Catch It, Check It, Change It."

> *Catch It:* Start to watch your thoughts about yourself and practice catching them. A lot of thoughts go by all day, but watch for those where you automatically think something negative about yourself. For example, after talking to someone new you might think, *This person will never be my friend because I'm trans. I'm never going to have any friends.* This is a pretty depressing thought, and most people would feel sad if they believed it. Show yourself some compassion for having this belief. Then move on to the next step.

> *Check It:* This is where you check out this thought. Is it really true that you'll never have any friends? Do you already have some friends? Do you know other TGD people who have friends? How likely is it that you will never have a friend? Not very!

> *Change It:* This is the step where you change what you think to make it more realistic; for example, *Even if this person doesn't like me, someone else will*; or *Many trans people have friends and I will too*; or

I already have great friends, and I'll make even more friends as time goes on.

That's it! You might write down these steps in your journal or download the worksheet at http://www.newharbinger.com/54193 so you can do them anytime.

Spiritual Self-Care

Spiritual self-care can help people feel a greater sense of peace and calm, increased meaning in life, and a sense of connection to something larger. For some people, spiritual self-care is connected to religion, but for many people it's not. It can really involve anything that grounds you and helps you feel centered, allowing you to better focus on your real self, your values, and what matters deeply to you.

For some people, mindful meditation creates this space. In a nutshell, mindfulness involves being more present in the current moment, with acceptance. There are many ways to practice mindfulness; examples are easily available online and through social media, including mindful prayers from many different religions. Common ways include taking time to breathe or focusing on breathing, checking in with your senses (what do you see, hear, feel, smell, taste?), and bringing focus to what you're currently doing, rather than thinking about other things. Practicing mindfulness, in general, can have many mental and physical benefits, including lowering stress levels, emotional reactivity, and symptoms of depression and anxiety. This increased sense of calm from practicing mindfulness can create that space to tune into what really matters to you. You might start by taking a few minutes right now to take the deepest breaths you have taken today and be present—really present—with yourself. We encourage you to look into meditation and mindfulness resources if you feel like this is for you. There are many resources for mindfulness for people of color, LGBTQ people,

TGD people, neurodiverse people, and those who have experienced trauma. There are also many approaches, so if one doesn't work for you—you already know what we're going to say—move on and look for what fits!

Connection to something bigger than yourself is central for many people in their spiritual self-care. This connection could be to other people sharing a spiritual experience, to a higher power through prayer, or to non-human living things (animals, nature). However you experience this connection is valid, so make space for it in your spiritual self-care.

Lastly, gratitude is an important part of spiritual self-care for many people in many traditions, including for your authors. Gratitude practices have been shown to have a number of physical and mental health benefits, including reduced stress, depression, and anxiety, and improved sleep. It's so easy to forget the good things we have when we feel down or have a bad experience. You can try thinking about what you're grateful for and writing it down in your journal. Be creative! You might include animals, nature, games, people, your health, your body, an object, or anything else you can think of. The wind blowing when you're too hot is an amazing thing to be grateful for! We recommend you do this gratitude practice every day and come back to those lists when you feel hopeless, lonely, or sad.

Self-Care at School

School can sometimes be a difficult place for trans youth, especially when it's a place where they're not being affirmed for who they are or they're being mistreated for who they are. If you're in this situation, you may need to increase your self-care around school. You can start by identifying allies among your peers, teachers, school staff, and school counselors. You might identify allies among your peers by paying attention to who else identifies on the LGBTQ+ spectrum and to kids who talk about valuing human rights. Look for the adults who display safe-space stickers or pride flags, who regularly use your correct name and pronouns, or who sponsor the school pride club. Once you identify allies in your environment, you can reach out to these supportive people to strategize how to best address negative interactions you're dealing with at school.

Whenever possible, minimize exposure to people who don't support or recognize your identity. This may involve changing classes or avoiding certain situations. A school counselor may be able to help you figure out a plan for leaving toxic environments, which are situations that harm you emotionally or physically. For example, they could give you a pass to leave class and go to the counseling office when you're experiencing distress. As always, seek help from a trusted adult if you're experiencing harassment, bullying, violence, or threats.

Another way to increase your self-care is to be gentle with yourself around the academic part of school. Sometimes it's really hard to work up to our potential when we're in negative environments. You deserve to have a good balance between schoolwork and life. It's more important that you survive than it is to get straight As.

Self-Care on Social Media

While social media can be a place where trans youth find support and affirmation, it can also be a place where youth can be harassed, get pulled into arguments about trans rights, and be involved in relationships that feel toxic. While we encourage you to continue to connect to the places that feel supportive and energizing, we also encourage you to disengage from social media platforms and relationships that are having a negative effect on you. Do your best to avoid arguing and avoid negative messages. Remember, social media is designed to be addictive and to keep us coming back to argue with others. Defending your identity on social media may feel important, but if it's making you feel more angry, more anxious, or worse about yourself, just disconnect. We're certain that the people online are not going to change their minds.

Social media is also a place where trans people sometimes compare themselves to other trans people and receive messages about not being trans enough, masculine enough, or feminine enough. These comparisons will not help you develop a positive sense of yourself, so stop engaging! Check on your feelings after being in online spaces: ask yourself, *How am I feeling about myself now compared to before I got online today? Am I feeling better or worse about my gender identity or expression?* If you're feeling worse, this is a sign that the messages you got during the experience are not healthy for you. In these cases, we suggest you eliminate or, at least, limit your access to these spaces that cause you to feel bad about yourself.

Self-Care with Nonaffirming Others

If your life involves family members and others in your communities who are not affirming your identity (for example, they're using the wrong name and pronouns or not seeing your trans identity as valid), it's normal to experience pain and anger about this. This is definitely a situation where you will need to increase self-care so that you're less injured by these assaults. What to do when people use the wrong name and pronouns is sometimes a tough decision to make. You might ask yourself, *Should I correct them or should I ignore it?* Correcting people takes energy, so you need to figure out if that energy is worth it. If you have already corrected this person a bunch of times, and they still are not gendering you correctly, you may feel like it's not worth continuing to correct them, or that it hurts even more after every failed attempt. It's okay to sometimes choose not to fight the fight if it will cause you more harm than good. So in this case, self-care would be to ignore the misgendering.

Another example is dealing with people who are loving but keep making mistakes. For some, you may really need to keep working on correcting them. Others (like your great-aunt who you only see once a year and who doesn't hear that well anymore) you might just let go because the effort is not worth it.

If you choose not to correct certain people any longer but still want things to change, a good way to care for yourself would be to ask for help from an ally. For example, maybe a supportive sibling could help with correcting your parents, adding to your self-care by giving you a break from doing all the emotional labor. Another strategy for self-care while dealing with nonaffirming others is to create boundaries. You might find you need to distance yourself from people who are not affirmative. It can also be helpful to be aware of the people who are affirmative, so you can seek support from them after these identity assaults.

Self-Care When You're Neurodivergent

If you're someone who has been diagnosed with neurodivergence (that is, autism spectrum, ADHD), or even if you haven't been diagnosed but identify with neurodivergent experiences, you may have some additional needs when it comes to self-care. It's common for neurodivergent people to experience feeling overwhelmed and overstimulated in social situations. These feelings can create a lot of anxiety and prevent people from being able to function effectively, so these situations require extra self-care. Think about increasing awareness of your senses so that you can become more aware of what it feels like when you're beginning to become overwhelmed; for example, *When there's a lot of noise, I feel my heart rate going up and my brain becomes foggy.* When you're in those situations, consider using noise-canceling headphones, leaving or limiting these overstimulating situations, bringing fidgets with you, and/or finding a place to take alone or quiet time.

Another challenge often faced by neurodivergent people is trying to fit into the social norms of neurotypical people. Neurodivergent people often refer to this as *masking,* and it can be exhausting! Therefore, it's important to find spaces to unmask, maybe by yourself and maybe with trusted friends and loved ones who understand your neurodivergence. Remember, being neurodivergent is just a difference in the way your brain works, not something that is wrong with you. And as mentioned in other sections, it's important to share your needs with trusted people so they can help advocate for you and support you in your challenges.

FROM SELF-HARM TO SELF-CARE

When we're under a lot of stress, we all rely on *coping strategies*, which are actions or thoughts we use to get through difficult situations. It's common for people to sometimes lean on coping strategies that feel good in the moment, but don't benefit us—and may even harm us—in the long run. For example, using drugs or alcohol can be a temporary relief or escape from our problems, but long-term use can cause health problems, increase our involvement in unsafe situations, and actually make depression and anxiety a lot worse. Sometimes when people are engaging in coping strategies they know are not healthy for their mind and body, they can develop shame about these behaviors. For example, when people seek relief through cutting or other self-harming behavior, they often feel like they have done something wrong and try to cover up their cuts, burns, and other evidence.

If you're using self-harming coping strategies, we're not here to judge. We encourage you to not be super hard on yourself and to reduce your self-judgment around these behaviors. Moving from the coping strategies you're familiar with to strategies that are good for your mental and physical health is a process. The idea is to explore new self-care options, including the ones discussed in this chapter, and gradually replace self-harming strategies with self-care.

Self-harming coping strategies are dangerous and can even lead to death, so we certainly don't wish for you to use these strategies. If you haven't used self-harming strategies, please don't start! It's better to not develop harmful habits in the first place. Instead, please use the self-care strategies in this chapter. Over time, people using self-harming strategies usually realize that those strategies were not what they really wanted for themselves because of the consequences and long-term harm these strategies have caused. All that said, we know that sometimes young people are going to use self-harming coping strategies. If you're choosing to self-harm, please remember that the point is for you to stay alive to do something different in the future. Therefore it's important that you consider your safety and reduce the harm that can come from these strategies.

One way to reduce the danger of self-harm is to try to delay the actual behavior. If you can slow down the action, you may be able to get to a more stable emotional place where you have more control over the situation. This control could lead to you choosing not to self-harm or to take a less dangerous approach in your self-harming behavior. When you get the urge to engage in a self-harming coping strategy, try to give yourself a set amount of time to wait until you do it, even if it's just five minutes. During that time, try some of the self-care ideas in this chapter to see if you can reduce or disarm the urge. You can also try to distract yourself or think of a less dangerous way to get a similar sensation. For example, instead of cutting, some people use ice to create an intense sensation without the danger of cutting. If you make it to the end of the five minutes and feel like you can wait longer, set another time goal. With this strategy, you may not be able to completely avoid self-harm, but you may be able to keep yourself safer.

Another strategy for reducing the danger of self-harm is to know what your triggers are. What are the situations, people, places, or times that create your urge to self-harm? And what does it feel like as these urges come on and increase? Do you have certain sensations in your body or typical thoughts when you're feeling the urge to self-harm? If you can gain awareness of what triggers you and what it feels like, it may help you slow down the process. Awareness may also give you information that allows you to avoid or leave triggering situations, or to seek support when you're in triggering situations.

Sometimes all the self-care in the world is not enough for us to feel healthy and happy. Or maybe we're feeling so unhealthy and unhappy, it makes it hard to even get a start on self-care. If you might be in this situation, it's important to look out for some of the red flags that are telling you that you need to seek care outside yourself. See chapter 1 for more details about these warning signs that you should seek help.

SQUAD CARE

Most of the talk about self-care so far has been focused on what you, as an individual, need to stay mentally, emotionally, and physically healthy. We mentioned earlier that Black queer feminist Audre Lorde (1988) thought of self-care as self-preservation and political warfare. As part of her idea, she also viewed self-care in a collective way, thinking of it as a community effort. We will refer to this idea as "squad care," which is a way of thinking about self-care as a process of building and nurturing supportive relationships. These supportive people make up your squad. This squad is different from a friend group; it's a community of people invested in your health and happiness. Being a part of a community like this has many benefits. It can give you a sense of belonging, safety, and empowerment; it can help relieve stress; and it can ultimately help you build resilience.

When you're connected to your squad, whether giving to it or leaning on it, you'll likely feel recharged, rewarded, and fulfilled. Think about how much better you feel after calling on a friend after a difficult day. And it also can feel good to be there for a friend after their difficult day.

To begin building your squad and identifying its potential members, you may find it helpful to think about the varying roles that different squad members might play. Your squad may be composed of a number of different relationships, such as:

- A family member who affirms your identity

- A trans/queer peer you can relate to through shared trans and queer experiences

- A mentor (possibly an older trans/queer person) who can share in your vulnerable moments and add insight based on their experiences

- A mentee who needs your support (helping them in their journey can allow you to reflect on your past experiences, which can be helpful in learning from your past and guiding your future goals)

- A friend who knows you well

- An ally who will stand up for you and advocate for you

- A trans-affirmative therapist

- Someone you're religiously and/or spiritually connected to

- A teammate, training partner, or someone who engages in a hobby with you

When thinking about these different roles, consider who is on your squad currently and how your squad may need to grow. Start by making a list in your journal of the people who are on your squad, and then asking yourself these questions:

Are there any relationships that need to change or be adjusted?

Are there any areas I wish were represented differently or more?

Do I feel heard and supported by the members of my squad?

What is my biggest need right now? Is it being met?

Take a moment to add to your journal any thoughts about how you want to be intentional about your squad: Who do you feel grateful for and why? Who has helped you feel comforted, supported, and cared for? What have they done to make you feel this way? What would you add or change? Consider sharing your gratitude and ideas as a way of feeding energy back into your squad.

Jade, who was eleven at the time of her interview, told us about how much she was struggling at school and how she used her squad (which she calls her team) to get through. She lived in a rural, politically conservative town, where people generally held negative beliefs about trans people. Jade wasn't yet out as a trans person, though she wore feminine clothes and had long hair. Kids would say things like, "You look like one of those weird kids who are going to get plastic surgery to look like a girl." And supposed friends would respond with, "Isn't that terrible that he's insulting you by saying you're one of *those* people?" Jade also faced challenges using the bathroom at school. Since she felt uncomfortable in both the girls' and boys' bathrooms, she was given permission to use the teachers' bathroom. Kids would question why she was using that bathroom and tell her she was not allowed to use it… geez, she was just trying to pee!

Jade used the support of her team to get through this tough time. She spoke to us of the importance of her team, which she described as, "A team of really important people that have helped me in my journey as a trans person, all of the people that I've talked to and shared my feelings." Her team included her parents, a therapist, a few close friends, and other trans/queer kids and adults who she met at the neighboring town's LGBTQ+

youth center. Jade's therapist helped her visualize her team's energy captured in a pretty pink rock. She would carry the rock with her to keep that supportive energy with her, especially for when she was coping with misgendering and mistreatment.

✦★ JADE'S STORY: A Little Rock of Resilience

This little rock is really important because when I hold it, I think of everyone that's helped me through my journey, they've helped me figure out who I am. They've just supported me a lot and it really helps to have a reminder that those people have always got my back. The rock is something to help me remember those people that I love and who love me, who support me and have helped me so much throughout my life. It's really important to me that I know those people are always at my side; if I ever need to talk to someone, they're right there.

At school, I was having trouble being a trans person because no one knew that I was trans so it was kind of hard because everyone saw me as a boy even though that's not who I was and that's not who I knew I was. But my team helped me talk to them and also gave me some strategies, like coping strategies, strategies to help myself tell them, "No, that's not who I am," and I've grown so much and learned so much, and my support team is a huge part of that. It definitely helped me.

There was a time when I was first starting to realize who I was and I was just so confused, I just couldn't figure it out. My team kind of stepped in and it made me feel so good. They helped me learn, they helped me improve. They helped me, not, sort of figure out who I was, because that was more of my job, but they definitely helped me through all that.

Jade also talked about how she's conscious of giving back to her team:

That's such an important part of me and my life and it's really hard to give back what they've given to me, but I try to show that I love them and that they're really helping me through my journey. I try to, not only with words, not only just saying thank you, but if they ever need a helping hand, I try to step in and help them since they've helped me so much. They really deserve that. Because they've given so much to me, I want to give back to them.

BOUNDARIES AND BALANCE IN RELATIONSHIPS

Sometimes we find ourselves in relationships where we feel that we give a lot and don't receive much in return. While it's natural to sometimes give more and receive less (like if a friend is going through a hard time), in the relationship overall, there should be a balance of giving and receiving. If you have a relationship like this, try asking yourself: *Over the last six months, what percentage of energy have I given and what percentage have I received?* If the answer is very unbalanced, this may require you to reevaluate this relationship and make new decisions around your boundaries in the relationship.

Boundaries are the rules and limits you set in relationships that are designed to keep these relationships healthy. Sometimes this means that the role a person plays in your life might shift over time, perhaps placing people who are draining to you in a more distant position in your life. Creating boundaries in your more draining relationships can open up space for relationships that feed your energy and support you in your challenges. After all, you deserve relationships in your life that provide you with comfort!

If you're thinking about setting new boundaries in a relationship, you might ask yourself, *How much exposure to this person is good for me?* You might decide that instead of texting a particular friend every day, a healthier level of contact is texting once a week. Your boundary in this case is weekly contact. You might decide to share that boundary with your friend, saying something like, "I really only have the emotional energy to talk once a week." Or you may just assert this boundary through actions, by only responding once a week. When you set a new boundary, it's common that people take some time to adjust to it. For example, your friend might keep texting you every day. In this case, it's up to you to maintain your boundary and respond only once a week. Remember that you have chosen that boundary to protect your mental health and that you deserve healthy relationships.

You're Worth It

Jade talked about asking for help as a first step to building a squad. She said, "Find someone you trust and let them know you're having a hard time. Ask them if they can help you with that." This is great advice, though sometimes it can feel really hard to ask for help. Sometimes people are afraid of being a burden to others, or they may feel they're not deserving of help. These self-critical thoughts can sometimes be even more complicated for trans people when they're dealing with internalized transphobia. For example, you might feel like you don't want to make the cisgender people in your life feel uncomfortable or inconvenienced by having to understand your needs as a trans person. This idea assumes that your needs as a trans person are less important or valid than the needs of cis people. It's understandable that you may feel that way because of the negative messages in society about trans people…but it's not true! Trans people are just as important as all other people, and they're deserving of care, just like everyone else.

Once you take that step to ask for help, you may also find it hard to receive that care. Again, the thoughts of being a burden or being undeserving may be swimming around in your head. Try to remind yourself that you deserve care, and let it in even when it feels uncomfortable. Imagine you're trying to help a friend who responds that they don't deserve it or that they're a burden. What would you say to them? We imagine you would say that they do deserve care and that they're not a burden. The same is true for you.

In summary, we encourage you to take good care of yourself. You deserve it! Identify the ways you already care for yourself and your squad, so you can be sure to maintain the strategies that are already working. Also, keep yourself open to exploring and finding new strategies for self-care. Next, we bounce forward to what to do when things get tough: how to cope with hard times in positive ways.

TAKEAWAYS

✸ Self-care refers to the day-to-day-things we do to stay mentally, emotionally, and physically healthy.

✸ Life can be difficult, so self-care needs to be part of our daily routine.

✸ Make it a regular practice to check in with yourself about how you're doing, and to increase your self-care when you're struggling.

✸ Self-care can be thought of as having three domains: physical self-care (taking care of your body); emotional self-care (caring for your mental health); and spiritual self-care (getting grounded in your real self, your values, and what really matters to you).

✸ You may require increased self-care when school is a difficult place to be; social media is causing you stress; other people are not affirming your gender; or aspects of neurodivergence make social situations difficult.

✸ Squad care is building and nurturing supportive relationships that can give you a sense of belonging, safety, and empowerment; help relieve stress; and help you build resilience.

CHAPTER 5

POSITIVE COPING: NEW WAYS TO GET THROUGH TOUGH TIMES

We've already talked about how transphobia, dysphoria, and the stress of other identities can add up to cause a lot of rough times for TGD youth. Along the way in this book you've learned about resilience, self-compassion, making friends with your body, and how to take better care of yourself every day. But what do you do when things get extra hard? If you're overwhelmed with negative thoughts and feelings to the point where you're not doing okay in your everyday life, obviously we hope that you're getting help from trusted, supportive adults. But even then, most of us need good ways to get through extra tough times. When we feel awful, this is when we need to bring in super-coping. We think of it as self-care on steroids, or what you can do in the short run to feel better in the long run.

Coping is what people do to manage stress and upset when things are overwhelming. Some kinds of coping that people do might feel good at first, but over time cause harm. Some kinds help you get through a tough time without making it worse, and that is what we will focus on.

SHORT-TERM COPING CAN LEAD TO PROBLEMS

Drinking, overeating, or using drugs are pretty common ways that people help themselves feel better in the short run. There are things we all do to avoid our bad feelings, like spacing out on our phones, playing video games, or sleeping a lot. Some people pick fights with friends and family, take risks like driving too fast, or use cutting or other types of self-harm. We don't judge you for using any of these at times. Some of them, like watching TV or being on your phone, are also just regular ways of having fun. Sometimes short-term solutions can be fine. For example, if you had an awful day at school and failed a test, you might decide to cope by just zoning out on your phone for a while in the evening.

The problem is when short-term solutions keep you from solving a problem or they make your problems worse. Most short-term solutions are meant to help us avoid or ignore the problem, hoping it goes away. But things that help us avoid can also be harmful, and ignoring problems rarely makes them go away. If you were to scroll on your phone all evening to avoid the stress of school, you might study even less and fail your next test, making school even more stressful. So how do you get through tough times without making things worse? This chapter is about trying new ways to feel better when you feel awful, so you can move on to figuring out how to solve problems or live more peacefully with them, not just avoid them.

START WITH THE BASICS

It sounds like a cliche, but the reality is that the basics really do make a difference. If you're having a rough time, always be sure to check these things first:

Hydration: It's in all the memes but being even a little dehydrated really does cause anxiety!

Eating: Often when we feel bad, we don't eat. Guess what? That makes you feel worse. Have a snack.

Sleep: Sure, you can get by on four hours of sleep. Kind of. Lack of sleep is directly related to more anxiety, and less ability to get emotions balanced. If needed, take even a short nap and see if that helps.

Sunlight: We really are like plants with feelings. Heading outside and getting some sun can really help your mood.

Movement: Literally just change locations or get some exercise. Any movement can help your mood but intense exercise can really turn a mood around.

Seeing a friend: Even a quick text exchange, a call, or seeing a friend in person can remind you that you're not alone.

These things won't solve big problems but they can really help you get perspective. If you're still struggling, try these next suggestions to calm your mind and body, practice acceptance, and change what you can. These are all ways that won't hurt and might help in trying to cope with a situation.

CALMING YOURSELF

One of the most important first steps to coping is to accept what's happening. Because life can be hard, having resilience has to include a level of acceptance that the world sucks in many ways. That is, there are things we cannot change or at least cannot change in the moment. Trying to change things that aren't changeable is like trying to walk through a wall. Even if that wall is in our way and we hate it and stay mad, we'll only hurt ourselves trying to walk through it. So you have to accept that the wall is there in order to figure out how to get around it—or find a new way through it. On the other hand, if we try to cope with it by ignoring or avoiding it, we might just be stuck on the wrong side of that wall forever.

Resilience doesn't mean that we avoid, or don't experience, heartache and pain. Instead it means being aware of the feelings that come up and helping yourself with those feelings until you can find a wise way to go forward. When you have good ways to cope, you can calm down your mind and body, take care of your mind and body, and then figure out what to do next. This chapter aims to help you practice building your ability to hang in there with hard feelings and find new ways to deal with moments of pain, anger, minority stress, and other life stress.

Regulating Your Body

When we're upset and in distress, our bodies react with physical responses. For example, we might feel our heart rate go up, our temperature rise, our stomach get painful or nauseous, or our breathing become difficult. Our bodies change in response to match our emotions. When we're in an upset state, it's not a good time to make decisions or take important action. These are times when we're usually not thinking clearly or rationally, and we may make decisions that are not what our true, centered self wants. Our emotions might want us to act without thinking. Even when there is no simple solution to the problem, we can at least try to get through the moment without making the situation worse.

In these stressful moments, it's important to work on getting our physical body back to a calm state. This is not to ignore it or act like nothing is happening, but rather to make sure our emotions aren't making the decisions. And, just as our body follows our emotions as they become elevated, our emotions will follow our body as it calms down. When this happens, we're better able to see what's happening and make the most effective choices.

The key is to slow down in those moments when we feel out of control. Many people find mindfulness activities—like meditation, yoga, breathing, coloring, connecting to nature, and many more—really useful. We wrote about this some in chapter 3.

Next, you'll read about two types of mindfulness activities that we think can be helpful in slowing down during moments of distress: breathing and grounding. We recommend practicing these exercises every day so that when things are hard and you feel upset, you'll be able to lean on them to help yourself out. The idea is not to be perfect, but to remind your mind and body that it is safe and good to slow down!

Breathing

One of the most effective calming strategies for the body is to focus on breathing, the very thing that keeps us alive. Remember, if we return to breathing calmly, we also invite our emotions to calm down. There is no one right way to practice calm breathing, but in general, these exercises encourage slow, even breaths that are deeper than your typical breaths. You want to feel both your lungs and abdomen fill with air. You should be able to see your chest inflate and your belly puff up a little.

Box breathing works especially well, and you can do it anywhere. This is when you breathe in for a count of four, hold your breath for a count of four, exhale for a count of four, and pause for a count of four...and then begin again. You can imagine you are breathing in up one side of the box, holding your breath across the top, breathing out down the other side, and pausing across the bottom. Repeat this cycle until you begin to feel your physical reactions start to slow down; it may take up to several minutes. Try to keep your attention on your breath and let go of your thinking. It's not always easy to do this when you feel upset, so don't feel discouraged if you find that your thoughts are wild and you forget about your breath. Just keep coming back to your breath and slowing down.

Grounding

Another helpful way to slow things down in moments of pain or distress is to use grounding exercises. These exercises are similar to breathing in that they help bring awareness to the present; for example, our physical surroundings and the physical safety of our bodies in the current moment. There are three types of grounding exercises: physical grounding, mental grounding, and soothing grounding. You can try these different types and use the techniques that work best for you.

Physical grounding techniques get you in touch with your senses. For example, try the 4, 3, 2, 1 exercise. Name four things you can see. Name three things you can hear. Name two things you can smell. Name one thing you can feel.

You can also try turning your attention to your body, possibly checking in with your posture, straightening your spine, rolling your shoulders back, and/or relaxing your face, including your jaw. Another strategy is changing your temperature. If intense emotion makes you feel hot, try splashing your face with cold water, holding an ice cube, using a wet washcloth to cool parts of your body, or sitting in front of a fan. If you tend to get cold, try a heated blanket or a warm bath. Finally, lying on the floor or ground and noticing where your body is supported can be helpful with physical grounding.

Mental grounding techniques provide you with a mental distraction to give you a little break from the intensity of your emotions. One idea is to think in categories; for example, try naming as many breeds of dogs as you can. When you have completed that, move to another category, like ice cream flavors. Another mental grounding strategy is describing things around you, being as detailed as possible. You can use all your senses—what you see, what you hear, and so on—in coming up with your description.

Soothing grounding techniques help you access things that you find comforting. For example, you might list your favorites: songs, colors, people, places, foods, and so on. You might also try picturing the face or voice of a person who supports you. You can think of what they would say to you in this tough moment; for example, *You're going to be okay. I'm here for you.* Just like breathing techniques, the more you practice grounding techniques, the easier it will be for you to remember to use them in moments of stress and high emotion.

IDENTIFYING WHAT IS AND IS NOT IN YOUR CONTROL

Once you have your body at least somewhat regulated, you can take a step back and observe the situation. *What's going on here? What can I do to change the situation? And what is out of my control?* Sometimes, we have little control over a situation. For example, we can't change what has already happened or control what other people do, say, or believe, such as transphobic thoughts and actions. While this can sometimes make us feel powerless, if we can accept the things that we can't change, it opens us up to see the things we *can* change.

Accepting what can't be changed can be a really hard (but necessary) step in regaining our sense of control, calming down, and ultimately building our resilience. Remember the metaphor of the wall we can't walk through? As long as we keep not accepting the wall, it kind of controls us—we end up hurting ourselves trying to fight it. But we regain control when we stop being controlled by anger or frustration and find a new way around the wall.

To do this, it can be helpful to repeat statements of acceptance either in your head or out loud, such as, "It is what it is," or "I can only control my own reactions and behaviors." You can also honor your feelings during this process. For example, you might think, *That person is a transphobe and I can't change that. What a jerk. Their behavior hurts others, including me.*

It can also be helpful to remind yourself that this situation or feeling is temporary. This reminder is particularly important if depression is a challenge for you. When we're in a dark place, depression often tells us that it has *always* been this way and that it will *always* be this way. Usually, this isn't true. Our moods and emotions, including symptoms of depression, tend to have their ups and downs.

Once we accept what we don't have control over, we can see more clearly what we can control. While we can't change what has already happened, we can choose how we respond. You can respond by either changing yourself or changing the problem. If we think about the wall, you could change yourself (Do you just need to get away from that wall for a bit and go in a different direction?) or the external problem (Do you need to learn how to build a door so you can go through the wall?).

Changing Yourself: Coping Without Harm

Mostly when we have a problem, we want it to go away *immediately*! But sometimes we can get through by helping ourselves just stay okay until things change, or even changing our mind about what is happening. But we have the most control over ourselves, and it's worth considering a few ideas.

Changing your environment. Sometimes situations are just too hard, and we need to get away from them. This can be especially important for neurodivergent folks who sometimes feel overstimulated and have a really hard time getting centered until the overstimulation stops. If you aren't going to be able to change Uncle Marcus's mind about pronouns, walking away from the conversation might be the best bet.

Distraction. Finding something to do to occupy your mind can give you a break from stewing about or overthinking your stressful situation. Some ideas are listening to music, watching funny videos, reading, watching upbeat shows or movies, and doing art or a project. There are so many sources of distraction, and we encourage you to find what works for you.

Visualizing a safe place. Remember visualizing a comforting place from chapter 3? Picture that place or another that you feel very safe in. Imagine it in as much detail as possible. What does this place look like? Are there smells or sounds you associate with this space?

Setting emotions aside. Sometimes it's too much to deal with emotions in the moment, so we can be intentional about setting them aside for the time being. You can even picture placing them in a box and putting them away on a shelf. You can always come back to them later when you're ready.

Looking for a silver lining. While it can be hard to think about the positive aspects of a stressful situation, it's true that we often grow through our tough times. For example, you might realize that you survived this situation, which can give you more confidence for the next stressful situation. Or you might think, *Well, now that I know that person is harmful to me, I know not to trust them again.*

Doing intense exercise to match your intense emotions. If there are ways you can exercise without it causing too much dysphoria, this can be a really great way to help process your emotions. One of your authors, Deb, is intentional about doing kickboxing on a regular basis. She often says, "I need to punch and kick things to survive the world!" Feelings of anger and even rage are valid emotions when you're facing mistreatment and injustice. Let it out in a healthy way so it doesn't eat you alive.

Changing your mind. Ask yourself if this is really the problem you want to tackle right now or if the person or thing is worth being upset about. For example, there is so much truly transphobic stuff on the internet that you could spend all day being upset, scared, and angry. Engaging with it only makes us feel more hopeless. But is some stranger on the internet really worth spending your energy on? Sometimes it's worth just deciding that it's *not* worth your time.

Asking for help. Sometimes just connecting with caring others is the most helpful thing. Even without talking about your problem (although that can be great too!), being around people who care about you can be soothing, help you see that there is more to the world than your problem, and remind you that you're not alone.

Changing the Problem

After you've regulated your body and changed what you can about your stressful situation, you can now use both your thoughts and emotions to decide how to proceed. The idea is that once we get more centered, we can make decisions that are as effective as possible for what we want and need. You might start by asking yourself, *What do I really need right now? What is important to me? What is the most effective thing I can do?*

When we're in our more centered place, we're better able to face our problems. Facing our problems often involves communicating with others about our feelings. It's healthy to be able to express to others what's going on inside us. Whatever you're feeling is important, so centered communication involves valuing yourself and knowing that your feelings and thoughts matter. However, we also need to take into account the other person or people involved, expressing our feelings in ways that are not harmful to them. When we can consider our own emotions important and communicate about them in ways that show respect for other people, it allows space for relationships to get stronger. That's ultimately what we want, since healthy relationships are very important in building resilience.

Let's think about what this could look like after a stressful situation. Let's say someone misgendered you, which increased your feelings of dysphoria and distress. When thinking about how to proceed from a centered place, you can first consider yourself and how you're feeling. You may identify feeling hurt, invalidated, and unsafe as a result of being misgendered. And then you can think about the person who misgendered you and what they're thinking and feeling. Maybe this person has good intentions in their relationship with you, and they're still learning how to be respectful of trans people. Maybe they would feel bad about hurting you. In a case like this, when you think about the relationship between you and the other person, it may feel worth sharing your feelings with this person to strengthen the relationship.

A helpful strategy for communication that is respectful of both your feelings and others' feelings is using what are called I-statements. These are statements where you talk about yourself, not the other person. I-statements sound like this: "I felt (insert emotion) when you (insert hurtful action)." So in the above situation, you might say, "I felt hurt, invalidated, and unsafe when you misgendered me. It's really important to me that you use my correct pronouns." When you start with your experience, clearly stating how you felt, your statement can often be heard more easily by others because it doesn't sound blaming and it gives a clear message of what you need going forward. This person now knows what you feel like when they use the wrong pronouns and may feel motivated to put more effort into using your correct pronouns. Remember to ask for you what you need! Saying only "I felt hurt when you pointed out where the men's room is to me" doesn't tell the other person "In the future, please remember that I only use the women's room."

Using I-statements and asking for what you need can take you a long way toward getting what you want. On the other hand, statements that accuse the other person or criticize too much can prevent you from getting what you want. The person may walk away from this interaction feeling more distant from you and less motivated to change their hurtful behavior.

Now let's think about another situation where someone misgendered you. This time, when you think about the other person's thoughts and feelings, you identify that this person has a pattern of being transphobic, and you don't believe their intentions are good. In this situation, you might decide that this isn't a relationship you want to invest in and that it wouldn't be safe for you to engage with that person. Here, your feelings are still important and you may decide to proceed in a different way. For example, you may talk to your friends, a teacher, or a school counselor about what happened, how you felt, and how you could try to avoid a similar situation in the future. Maybe you would decide to ask a teacher if you can move your seat away from the person who misgendered you, or ask a school counselor for a pass to leave class if this situation happens again. In these situations, your goal is not to strengthen the relationship with the harmful person, but to lean on your other healthy relationships.

LONG-TERM COPING: PLANT FLOWERS IN THE CORNERS

As we acknowledged earlier, the world is often a difficult place, so we also need coping strategies that serve us in the long run. To cultivate long-term coping, we encourage you to "plant flowers in the corners." These corners are the spaces we can retreat to when the stress of the world is too hard. For some of us, these flowers could literally be plants or flowers that we nurture and watch grow. But these flowers could take all kinds of different forms. The idea is that these are spaces we nurture so they're there for us when we need them.

So let's think about how you can grow these nurturing spaces. First, let's take a look at what leads people to feel more happiness. Many people are focused on goals that have external rewards, like money, image, and status. It's not surprising that we often think these things would make us happy. Our capitalist society teaches us that a lot of money, image, and status are what is most important. When people achieve these goals, they may feel excited for a short time, but these achievements don't typically bring long-term happiness.

On the other hand, some people focus more on intrinsic goals that are satisfying to their emotions, values, and wellness. These goals meet our basic needs as humans, such as personal growth, having close connected relationships, and having a feeling of community. People who focus more on these goals are happier in the long run and have less depression and anxiety. Chapter 7 will help you do a deep dive into identifying your values and thinking about how to build a life that has meaning to you. Meanwhile, keep watering those flowers: accepting yourself little by little; finding close, supportive friends; and building a strong community are all things that you'll be able to turn to in moments of crisis in the future. You probably don't have those three things where you want them to be right now but even the process of growing them will make you a more resilient person who is able to stay healthy, hopeful, and well, even during tough times.

EXISTENCE AS RESISTANCE

In many ways, TGD people demonstrate strength and resilience just by existing. Being TGD requires you to question society's way of thinking. The dominant message in society is that gender is binary and that sex assigned at birth determines gender. Therefore, just by identifying as TGD, you have already developed the strength to challenge what many other people see as truths. It takes strength to choose a path of congruence and authenticity. If you have chosen to share your TGD identity with others, you have had the courage to assert your truth, even though sometimes it's not met with support by family, peers, cultural or religious communities, and the larger society.

We encourage you to acknowledge this strength you already have inside you—it's very important to see our own positive traits as part of building resilience. We also believe that part of resilience is to resist the injustices that have caused us such pain. As a TGD youth, you're facing oppressive forces such as transphobia, mistreatment, rejection, invalidation, and even laws that take away your rights. As you move through the world as a TGD person, you're resisting these oppressive forces. While we know this can often feel like a burden, we encourage you to also see the contribution you're making to help the world stretch its thinking, making more space for all people to exist and be treated with kindness and compassion. Just by existing, you're resisting…thank you for making the world a better place.

TAKEAWAYS

* Some coping strategies can be helpful in the short run but not healthy in the long run. It's important to find coping strategies that get us through a situation without making it worse.

* When we're upset, our bodies often react physically. Before we respond in a situation, we need to first regulate our body and bring it back to a calm state. Mindfulness exercises, such as breathing and grounding, can help. Once we're calm, we can identify what we can change about the situation and what we can't change.

* Accepting what we can't change can be hard, but it's important. Change what you can about the situation, such as leaving the stressful environment or finding a distraction.

* Acknowledge that your feelings are important and communicate those feelings in a respectful way; for example, by using I-statements: "I felt (insert emotion) when you (insert hurtful action)." Then, ask for the thing you need the person to do in the future.

* Develop long-term coping strategies by nurturing things that bring you comfort—your flowers in the corners of life—so you have somewhere to go when things get hard.

* Finding ways to be who you really are, nurturing relationships, and having a sense of community are common things that can provide comfort when you need it.

* As a TGD person, you're challenging society's way of thinking and that takes strength!

CHAPTER 6

COMMUNITY, BELONGING, AND RESISTANCE

For everything you eat or drink, there are many people who have been an important part of getting that food or drink to you. Without other people alongside us, it becomes very hard to get our basic needs met. Even though we might see that people can also do harmful things to each other, the fact is that we need each other in order to be healthy and well.

Our connections to other people are also important for our mental health and well-being. In fact, well-known psychologist Abraham Maslow (1943) drew a pyramid of our human needs. In the pyramid, our needs like food, water, and shelter are near the base, as we need them first to survive. But the next most important thing we need, Maslow said, is a sense of belonging. Feeling that we belong is important to our mental health and emotional well-being. Feeling that we belong makes us feel supported and safe. Feeling connection with others can also give us a sense of meaning in life. When we feel connected to others, we can contribute to supporting others around us, and this can also make us feel good.

This need for connection is doubly true for TGD people. One of the most important ways that TGD youth can stay strong and resilient is by finding a solid community. Despite all the ways you might feel rejected or mistreated by the world, a strong community can act like bubble wrap, protecting you against these things. In this chapter, we will focus on how to create meaningful relationships that can last over time and how to find connection to communities of people who support and care about each other.

BELONGING AS A TGD PERSON

You might find it interesting that being TGD can make it both harder and easier to find a sense of belonging. While it's true that TGD people may find it harder to find others who understand and support you, there are ways that having these identities can actually *improve* your sense of belonging as well. How? For one, the journey to explore your gender can make you wiser, stronger, more courageous, and most importantly, more able to be your true self. When we know ourselves in this deeper way, we can be more of our true selves in our relationships, which can help us develop stronger relationships with others. It feels great to find people you can be your true self around! And you can return that gift by being accepting of someone else's true self. Being TGD might help someone else find a sense of belonging in a TGD, LGBTQ+, or queer community. Even more broadly, TGD people say they find belonging in larger groups of people who also care about making social changes, striving to make things more fair for people of all different identities.

Let's explore how being TGD can affect our sense of belonging a bit more. We'll start by looking at the ways being TGD can create blocks to feeling like you belong. Then we'll take a look at all the ways *you* can create a sense of belonging, including by forming relationships with the right people for you, making your relationships stronger, and also connecting to larger communities who share your identities or interests.

Why Is It So Hard to Belong?

TGD people may often feel—and worry—that they don't belong. This is for a good reason: family members, people at school, social media, religious leaders, and even politicians can send signs that you don't belong. For example, if a friend stops talking to you right after you tell them you're nonbinary, it's pretty normal that you would wonder if they're rejecting you. If a pastor at church says that TGD people are not following the teachings of the church, you may feel that you no longer belong there. Or if someone says you shouldn't be allowed to be on the sports team you're on because of your gender, you may feel like they're saying you aren't wanted there. Those are all clear examples of rejection.

However, feeling like you don't belong can also happen following things that are not so obvious. For example, let's say you're at a wedding and the photographer says, "Okay, let's get a photo with all the men and then one with all the ladies," and no one in your family says anything about that not including you as a nonbinary person. Non-TGD people may see this as no big deal, but it still can make someone feel like they don't belong in their family. Or if your friend laughs at a mean joke about trans people and then says, "Oh, but not you," you're getting a message that this person doesn't really understand you, even if they're your friend.

In some situations, it can be super confusing when you aren't sure why something happened and whether it has to do with being TGD. For example, if someone you meet seems like they're not interested in talking to you, you could draw many conclusions. You might think they're just having a bad day, or you could think they're shy, or you could think they're judging your gender or the way you dress. This question about what someone is thinking about you and why they're not being friendly to you can create a huge amount of stress, as well as a feeling that you don't belong.

If your culture has sent negative messages about being trans throughout your whole life, you naturally start to believe some negative things about yourself. We talked about this previously as internalized transphobia. It's not your fault that you took in these messages, and they can cause some unfortunate things for TGD people. Let's look at an example. Maybe you've been hearing about other TGD people facing things like rejection, nonaffirmation, violence, and discrimination on social media or the news. Naturally you'll start to be worried that this is going to happen to you. It makes sense to be extra alert because these things can happen. And it's hard on your mind and body to always be alert!

If you have been hearing negative things about TGD people, like that there is something bad about them, it's also normal that you might become less confident in yourself if you're a TGD person. This can happen even if you don't really believe there is anything wrong with being TGD.

From all these messages, it makes sense you would start to expect to be judged by others, and become a bit fearful or down about being around other people. You might decide because you're nervous or feeling down that you don't want to go to a party or that you don't want to go to college or that you don't want to try dating. Or you might try some of these things, but be more likely to be quiet and shy, out of a desire to protect yourself. This all makes so much sense. In fact, it might be smart to protect ourselves in some situations. But this is so tricky, because when we don't meet people, we never get an opportunity to meet really great people! So, sadly, the messages we get from the world can make us more fearful and less confident, and then we never get a chance to form community.

Being TGD isn't the only reason why it might be hard to feel connected to others. For example, people who are neurodivergent might find that figuring out what is expected in social situations is really confusing, anxiety provoking, frustrating, or overwhelming. And they may feel misunderstood by others, especially by neurotypical people. If you feel like this is true for you, it can be really helpful to find some online (or in person) support groups of people who share your experience, and also to find a therapist who really gets it, so they can help you find ways to connect with those around you who feel good.

Rowan, a nineteen-year-old who identifies as a trans guy and neurodivergent, has had this experience and has found some people who really let him be himself. Let's hear what he has to say about finding friendship and belonging.

✦★ ROWAN'S STORY

I'm really close to my best friend, who's trans as well. We've been best friends for eight years. He's not neurodivergent, he doesn't have ADHD or autism like me, and the way that he perceives stuff versus the way that I perceive stuff can vary, and it's never been a problem for our friendship, but I've realized my comfort level around him sometimes makes it hard to fully unmask. And recently I've become a lot closer with another best friend. He's not replacing my other one, but he's like the same exact flavor of neurospicy, and we're always on the same page. It's fantastic because we totally get to relax around each other. I haven't had an outlet for my ADHD energy since I was a kid, so having somebody else who really gets it, it helps me offset that energy that gets built up from living in a society that's so not built for you. So find a safe space, a safe person, a safe activity, something that helps you offset that energy. Look into being friends with people you wouldn't normally be friends with because maybe they get you on a level you haven't experienced before. I've never been friends with somebody like my new best friend but we're really close. So don't be afraid to look around for people who really get you. They're worth it, even if they're more effort or more out of the way.

FINDING BELONGING

We loved what Rowan taught us about how different friends can give us different things. And sometimes we need to have a few friends like he did to be sure that someone really understood his flavor of neurospicy. Similarly, you might look back at the "squad care" section of your journal to read about how you want to expand the group of people in your squad.

So how can you build, strengthen, and maintain connections with people that feel good? How can you find relationships that make you feel safe and supported, and that give you a sense of happiness and well-being?

Building Community with Other Trans and Nonbinary People

As we said earlier, being TGD isn't always a bad thing for finding people and places where you belong. In fact, having a TGD identity can be a way that people find belonging. Throughout history, people of color, cultural groups, and religions have come together to form communities full of joy, strength, and resilience. For many TGD people, their relationships with other TGD people become incredible resources for them to feel whole and safe and good about themselves, as well as to not feel alone. People who share your identity will often have some shared experiences. They will understand things that others don't, like how it feels to be in a body like yours, what it's like to deal with coming out to people, and how it is to start dating as a TGD person. Together, it can be easier to build a sense of community pride. TGD people have done amazing things and are helping free everyone from being trapped in gender boxes. Being with others who share your identity also helps you feel stronger when life gets hard. For example, if you start to worry that you'll be rejected for being TGD at a new job, it might feel much less scary if you know you have some TGD friends who are going to understand and remind you how awesome you are if that happens.

Connecting with the TGD community can also help you build self-compassion, self-respect, and hope. When you can see that you have amazing, smart, funny TGD friends, and you see that there's nothing wrong with them, it's easier to see that there is nothing wrong with you. Seeing examples of people who are happy and healthy in your community makes it easier to hold hope for yourself. TGD community spaces can also be safe places to experiment with or enjoy using different names, pronouns, dress, and other gender expressions to see what feels good to you. As part of the TGD community, over time you can also help create a safe space for others like you to feel seen and heard for who they are. When you do this, it can feel really great to know you're doing something meaningful and important.

You might start by looking for events, clubs, or online groups. You can search local papers, meetup groups, or social media postings, or ask someone who is part of your community. Maybe there is a queer hiking group or a pride barbeque or a dance party or a TGD summer camp? Even for people who don't have a lot of other TGD people in their local area, or money to travel, there are many online communities. So connecting to a TGD community is possible for most people in some way. It's important when you choose any community, in person or online, that you "take the temperature" the first few times you go. You want to see whether the community seems like one where everyone can feel safe and where all people and experiences are treated with respect. Add your energy to communities that feel good and safe for everyone. That will help them grow and expand. You may also encounter spaces that seem like they have problems as you search around. While it can be tempting to try to change, or argue with, people in spaces that seem like they have problems, our general recommendation for building resilience is to spend your energy contributing to spaces that seem to have a good feeling.

Expanding Your Community

You might find that you need different types of communities at different times in your life. Many TGD people find it really important to surround themselves with other TGD people as they're starting to explore and understand that they're TGD. It can be totally normal for someone to want to hang out just with other TGD people, and to only feel really comfortable and like themselves around other TGD people for a period of time. For example, you might feel like you're not really as interested in hanging out with some old friends who are cisgender and straight. You might even find yourself feeling annoyed or bored around them, but not have any reason to explain why. You might find yourself feeling kind of alone even when you're around them. When this happens, it can be hard for the TGD person and sometimes also for others around them who don't really understand. Friends and family might become concerned or judgmental that the TGD person seems to be changing and wants to be hanging out with other people or doing other things now. If you do find yourself feeling connected only to other TGD people and not interested in hanging out with old friends, we want to let you know that this can be normal, and even healthy, for a period of time. However, it doesn't mean you will always feel that way around your other friends.

While it's very normal and healthy to want to be around others who share your identity, that doesn't mean that TGD people can't feel they belong in other communities and groups. Like we said earlier, it's helpful to have a lot of different types of connections in our lives so that we're resilient even if one support we have isn't always available. Further, if you have other identities, such as cultural, religious, neurodiverse, or other types of identities that need support and community, having community outside being TGD can be so important!

Just like we suggested for finding new friendships, you can find new communities to connect with by figuring out what your interests or important identities are and then following those. Are there certain activities you like to do or certain things you care about? Maybe you like to learn how to build things, or your family's religion is important to you, or you feel strongly about animal rights. A great way to get involved with communities of others who share your interests can be to volunteer for something, join a club, or take a class outside of school.

For many TGD people, it can feel scary to go to a place without knowing how people there will react to your gender. Depending on where you live, it can be smart to be careful going into new communities. In these situations, we recommend a few things to help you stay safe. First, if you do have a friend or family member who can come with you the first time or the first few times, that can be super helpful. Second, you can call or email ahead, or have someone else you trust call or email for you, to ask any questions you have related to gender. For example, let's say you're really interested in martial arts. There's a martial arts dojo in your town, but you're feeling a bit scared to go. Are the classes divided by "boys" and "girls"? What will it be like if they have locker rooms to change in? Will you face any discrimination, nonaffirmation, or bullying there?

In this example, you might first call to ask some questions. You don't even need to tell them who you are. You can call without giving your name and say that you, or someone you know, is thinking about coming to a class, but you (or they) are TGD and wanted to know some things. You can ask questions like, "Are the teachers there supportive of people with TGD identities?"; "Are classes divided based on gender?"; and anything else you would like to know. This information will help you decide whether to go or not. It can be helpful to make these calls with someone who supports you nearby, just in case they say anything that makes you feel disappointed, hurt, or angry. Or you might even ask your friend or family member to call for you while you listen, if you're feeling nervous. If after talking to them, you think it does sounds like a good place for you to try out, you might still consider bringing a friend or family member with you the first time or two until you have a good sense of what the community is like. By taking steps like these, we can keep ourselves safe without cutting ourselves off from the possibilities of finding new communities where we feel a sense of belonging.

MEETING NEW FRIENDS

Now that you have some ideas about what kinds of communities you want to be a part of, and what kinds of friends you want to have, you might be wondering…how do you find TGD people just…out there? And how do you find other friends who don't share your identity but would be amazing, supportive people? We have a few ideas to help you get started.

Follow Your Interests

How do you even start finding people who might be accepting and supportive? Easy! By exploring what you *really* care about. What do you find fun? What's important to you? For example, since your author Ry likes to play music, wherever he goes, he looks for music groups to join and often finds some friends there. When you're doing things that you really enjoy and care about, people will be naturally interested in you. And, when you have some shared interests with someone, it's also easier to figure out how to invite them to hang out with you. If you both like to do art, why not do some art together?

Volunteering is a great way to find people who are also interested in helping others. There you're likely to meet other people who share your values. Love animals? Volunteering at the animal shelter, you're sure to meet other people who also really care about them. If you're neurodivergent, volunteering, a job, or helping a neighbor with a project can be ways to get to know people over time without a lot of pressure to act a certain way so you can "make friends." If you volunteer for something that matches your interests, other people there will want to talk about what you're already interested in.

Follow Your Gut

Shared interests and things you care about aren't all there is to finding a good friend. One of the easiest ways to tell who might be a good friend is to think about how you feel when you spend time with them and after you spend time with them. If you tend to feel more comfortable, safe, and happy than not, this is a reliable sign that a relationship is a good one.

Another thing to watch for is how they treat other people. Do they tend to keep the same friends around? Do they talk in kind ways about their other friends? Do they seem open to people who are different from them? Watch how they treat strangers too. Are they nice to the coffee shop workers? If someone you meet treats others respectfully, it's a good sign that they will treat you respectfully as well.

If your friend seems to be mistreating others, or worse, is mistreating you, it's best to start avoiding that person. You may feel like there aren't enough people out there to have better friends, but trust us, it's better to look for someone new than to tolerate meanness, bullying, or transphobia from a so-called friend. If you're being bullied, threatened, or harassed, it's time to get help from a trusted adult or call one of the crisis lines you'll find in our resources section. This kind of abuse can be harmful and should *not* be tolerated.

Test the Waters

If you're getting to know someone and you're not sure how they treat or react to TGD people, you might want to test the waters to learn more. After all, you're looking for people who are not only going to accept you for who you are but will also stand up for you. Watch for them to drop hints about movies, books, and their thoughts on gender, politics, or related events. Do they talk positively about a trans character in a TV show? If there's not a lot to go on, you could drop your own hints about movies or books or so on that have TGD content. If you hear or see something that sounds transphobic to you, that may be a sign that this is not someone you want to get closer to. Keep in mind that everyone can make minor mistakes about pronouns or misunderstand something about trans lives. You're listening for basic respect for TGD identities.

Figure Out What Type of Relationship You Both Want

Another thing to figure out when you're finding a possible new friend or other relationship is what type of relationship you want and whether the other person wants the same thing. Ask yourself, *Is this person someone I want as a friend I talk to every day, or just as more of a homework buddy, or as someone to date, or something else?* You might not know right away when you meet someone. You might need to get to know them a bit by spending more time with them before you can decide what type of relationship you want. You might think about whether they have the same interests as you and whether you feel good when you spend time with them, like we talked about earlier.

Once you know what type of relationship you want, it's important to figure out if they want the same thing. You can look for signs, like whether they respond to your messages right away, or how often they invite you to do things. If you're not sure what the other person wants, it can be helpful to just ask them; for example, "Hey, I had a lot of fun today. I hope we can hang out again soon. What do you think?" If you find out someone is not interested in the type of relationship you want (whether friendship, dating, or something else), it can be better to put your time and energy toward someone who does want the same thing as you.

Spread Out Your Support

It's smart to be connected to a few different people and communities. That way, if something disrupts one friendship or one friend group, you're not suddenly feeling all alone. Friendships, romances, and even family relationships are always changing and usually have their ups and downs—and coming out can sometimes cause some ups and downs in relationships. But if you have connections with more than one person or group, then you're more likely to continue to feel a sense of belonging as some relationships shift and change.

COMING OUT AS TGD

When we know ourselves better, we can choose to be more ourselves in our relationships. This can be true whether or not you're out to everyone. For many people, there will be times when coming out as TGD doesn't feel safe or like something they want to do. It's totally okay, and sometimes smart, to not be out. But coming out, when we decide it's right in a relationship, can be an opportunity for making our connection with that person stronger, even if it doesn't always seem that way at first. For many TGD people, relationships with others go through a difficult time when they first come out to them. People they used to rely on might suddenly start acting weird or even mean. And even if peers and friends are cool and get it, relationships with family can be really complicated. Coming out or being yourself might also feel hard in the communities you're in. For example, some TGD people feel like they have to choose between their TGD identity and their religious or cultural community. This can all be stressful.

There are quite a few books for LGBTQ+ youth on coming out, and if coming out to friends and family is what's next for you, we recommend you pick up one of those books, or look at other resources to help you plan for how to do this well. At http://www.newharbinger.com/54193, you'll find a list of these resources.

For some relationships, coming out will actually lead to a stronger connection over time. Sharing the harder things to talk about, and being more honest and vulnerable, can lead to relationships where people understand each other better, trust each other more, and feel more connected to each other. Of course, this doesn't always happen right away. Some people just don't get it or say things that are really hard to hear. But when we do value and trust a relationship enough to come out to someone, we give that relationship a chance to become even stronger. In other words, coming out can be not only a reason why relationships end, but also a reason why they become stronger.

KEEP IT GOING

Friendships and other relationships that last over time can be extra important and special. People who know each other over the years can help each other feel more stable and supported when things get stressful, as well as share joy in the good times. For TGD people, this can mean getting through some of the rougher moments with friends, family, and community.

Valuable relationships are sometimes tested when people don't quite understand your gender, don't get what it's like to be TGD, accidentally make harmful comments, or do other things that might make you feel rejected based on your gender. And, like we mentioned earlier, many TGD people are especially sensitive to rejection because of how often they hear negative and upsetting messages about themselves. This section is about how to get through those tough moments with people that you want to keep in your life. There are three parts to this.

Start with self-compassion. When you've encountered a tough time in a relationship, the place to start is with compassion for yourself. Go back to chapter 2 to review self-compassion and chapter 4 for self-care to try a few of the exercises. The point here is to validate your own feelings, take time to calm down your mind and body, and figure out what you need to feel better before talking to the other person.

Understand the other person. To really understand a person and help them understand us, we usually need to have a conversation instead of just guessing what they are feeling or thinking. So how do we do this well? It's all about being curious!

It can be helpful to tell the person what you heard them say and be curious about what they meant. This means not jumping to conclusions but staying open to the idea that there is more happening than you know. You can ask questions until you really understand the situation. Your friend might need something from you too, especially if you learn that you misunderstood something; in many conflicts, both people have missed some important point. For the moment, you'll need to be more curious than upset, so we recommend making sure you've been compassionate enough toward yourself to feel better before trying this.

Similarly, it can be helpful in hard conversations to ask the other person what they heard you say, to make sure they got the right message from your words. Finally, when a conversation is hard, it can be helpful to tell the other person, even if you don't agree or you feel hurt or angry, that you still care about them. And if you find yourself worried that the other person doesn't like you anymore, you can actually tell them what you're feeling. You can say, "Right now I'm feeling worried that, because of this conversation, you won't like me anymore." This can give you both a chance to see if you can care about each other, even through hard times. In healthy relationships, we can have a feeling like anger or hurt, but still know we care about each other.

Figure out what you need and ask for it. Finally, it can really help in any situation to ask for what we need from someone else, but first you need to figure out what that is. Sometimes we need an apology, or a reminder that a friend really cares for us. You may find yourself needing to make requests for people to try to use the right name or pronoun for you. So, after you've gotten clear what is happening for your friend, get clear about what you need. When you ask for what you need, try to do so in a respectful and calm way. This increases the chance that the person will want to give that to you.

Let's use the example of a situation where someone uses the wrong pronouns for you. After you've done what you need to take care of yourself (talk to a friend, exercise, and so on) you might start a conversation with this person. We recommend that, whenever possible, you avoid doing this by text; try to meet in person instead. You want to make sure you really get each other and feel good around each other. When you do talk with the person, it can be helpful to start by sharing your experience of what you remember happening, what you thought, and how you felt. Then you can ask them about their experience; for example, "Hi, Marta. I wanted to talk to you about yesterday. When you told Evan I'd be late, you used 'he' for me, but you know my pronouns are they/them. It felt so uncomfortable, and I was angry for a bit. I wanted to tell you that this was hard for me. And I'm curious about what happened on your side."

This is a good starting place for coming together in an honest conversation. Let's say Marta says, "Oh, I got nervous and I slipped up and I feel really bad." What do you need next? Each person is different, so whatever you need is okay, but one possible response is: "I totally get it, and I know you feel bad. I'd really appreciate it if you'd be willing to practice using my pronouns so you get it right more often." Or you could say, "You usually get my pronouns right, but now I'm worried that Evan might use the wrong pronouns. Could you text him and correct yourself?" Of course, if your friend responds in a way that seems angry or mean, then you might have a different set of needs that would sound like this: "Marta, this is important to me, and I need more respect for my identity."

Misgendering can be a pretty common experience for TGD people. Whether it's using the wrong pronoun or the wrong name or mixing up what your gender is, misgendering is the source of a lot of relationship stress. So let's go back to get some advice from Rowan.

⁺★ ROWAN'S STORY: Misgendering

There's a spectrum when it comes to the kind of people you deal with, like somebody I deal with at work and don't see that much, not that high of a priority. But when it's someone like a parent, a family member, a partner, anybody who's really close to your life, those people hurt the most, and those relationships can be the hardest to mend. Like my dad was really hard to bring around. It took him like two years to consistently gender me correctly after I came out.

It's tough. You have to decide if you're going to be vulnerable with them and give them a chance to grow or if you're going to protect yourself and just tough it out. I honestly think that it has to go in cycles when it comes to people you're close with. Like a cycle of being vulnerable and trying to teach them, and have them hear you and understand why it's important to do this. They sometimes don't understand why it's important, and it might not be out of direct disrespect but they end up disrespecting you. I feel like you have to go through cycles of repairing yourself from that taxing effort of proving your identity to somebody and just asking for basic human respect. It's really tough to balance all that, so you have to take a break, step back. Like if my dad misgenders me, I just tune it out and kind of emotionally block that because it's negative energy that's hard to take in.

With negative energy, the two options I see are you can protect yourself from it and avoid it, or you can use your own energy to try to spin it to a more positive light. It's an important skill to have, but it's exhausting. You can't do it 24/7 when there's so much negative energy around.

When it comes down to it, you can deliver your message however you want and ask for the respect you deserve, but some people don't listen to anybody. So you have to weigh those options in terms of the people you want to keep in your life and what's healthy and sustainable for you.

Here, Rowan talks about figuring out what he needs from different types of people. He discusses weighing the options and determining what is worth trying to ask for. He also reminds us that self-care is such an important part of these tough moments. Sometimes he decides that blocking it out is better, sometimes trying to make things more positive can help. In the end, taking care of yourself is going to help maintain the relationships you really want to keep because, as Rowan points out, having to defend yourself so much is tiring.

TGD COMMUNITIES AND SOCIAL CHANGE

Many TGD people choose to become a part of a community that helps make social change happen, so that all people are treated with respect, fairness, and kindness. Sometimes this happens inside TGD communities, and sometimes this means joining larger communities that fight for the rights of others. As people of different marginalized identities connect with each other and with allies, they become more powerful. It's easy to ignore one person who asks for change, but it's very difficult to ignore larger groups of people who ask for change. Together, we're more able to shift our communities and schools to be more welcoming places for all. The changes we have made over time to protect human rights show that change takes the energy of many people coming together.

Racism, Sexism, Ableism, and Other Prejudices

Racism, sexism, ableism, and other prejudices can still happen in TGD spaces. This means that TGD people of color, neurodivergent people, folks with disabilities, or those who come from poorer neighborhoods might feel discriminated against in some TGD groups. This can be especially hard for those who experience prejudice from one community for being TGD, and also racism from within the TGD community. These multiple discriminations can add up and make it hard for some people to feel like they belong anywhere.

Sexism and "binaryism" (preferring people who have binary identities) can appear even within TGD communities. A common example is that in some TGD communities, people can become very focused on "passing" (looking cisgender), and people who look the most masculine or feminine can be seen as better than others. Not only does this create pain for some, but it also leaves out a lot of nonbinary and gender diverse people who might not identify as "men" or "women." In other TGD communities, people who identify as nonbinary are in the majority, and people who feel more binary and use he/him or she/her pronouns can feel like their identities are judged.

If this is happening for you, we encourage you to keep looking. There are so many ways to connect online to specific groups and information, even if there aren't a lot of people right where you live who have the identities you do. However, no community is perfect, and if you're getting a lot out of yours, you may also decide to remain in the group or community and attempt to advocate for greater awareness of your needs and identities. This can be stressful, however, and each person needs to decide on a balance between trying to change a community and just needing to find one that works better for them.

Making a More Inclusive Community

In the end, it's up to us to help make sure that any communities we're a part of are safe and welcoming for others. Regardless of your identity, there is likely some other group who tends to be left out or even discriminated against in your community. We feel that part of being TGD means growing your sense of connection to all people who experience discrimination and using that experience to speak out for greater equality and inclusion for all people.

We can start by educating ourselves about the other ways that people experience discrimination and rejection. You've noticed us mentioning race, ability, body size, religion, neurodiversity, and more. There are other factors too, like how much money someone has or where they went to school. Use your experience as a TGD person (and your other marginalized identities) to imagine how that person must be feeling. We can each do our own part by reaching out to anyone who appears to be left out in a group, or by speaking up if we notice that something is said that doesn't create a welcoming space for all, or by correcting ourselves when we notice we've said or done something that could make someone else feel they don't belong. The more we can help create safe spaces for others, the more we'll find that these spaces give us a sense of safety and connection ourselves.

When we come together in communities, we feel less alone. We find that our lives are important to support each other. We can feel more confident that, in tough times, someone will still be there to support us. And we can find happiness in our ability to be there for someone else. We also find that together we have more power to create positive social change. Finally, it can be extra powerful to be a part of communities that care about making social change happen so that everyone feels they belong everywhere.

TAKEAWAYS

✳ Feeling connected to other people or communities can really help your resilience.

✳ Messages of rejection toward TGD people can create barriers to feeling like you belong.

✳ TGD people can also have "internal" blocks to finding belonging—like fear of how they will be treated by others, or lack of self-confidence —that make it hard to reach out for new connections.

✳ Good ways to form positive new connections include:

* finding others who are interested in the same things as you;

* trying to spend more time with people who you usually feel good around;

* avoiding people who bully you or harm you in other ways;

* getting help if you're being seriously bullied, harassed, or threatened; and

* figuring out if you and the other person want the same type of relationship.

✳ While we can't control how other people act or feel, we can build the skills we need to solve problems in long-lasting relationships by practicing three things: having understanding and compassion for ourselves, approaching the other person with curiosity, and determining what we need from the situation.

* Being TGD can create amazing opportunities to feel connected to others, by finding belonging in TGD, LGBTQ++, or queer communities. You can find these communities in person or online. You can "take the temperature" of different communities in your first few times hanging out with them, and then devote your energy to a community that feels good for you and others to feel safe in.

* It's normal for many TGD people to go through some times where they feel connected to only to other TGD people and communities.

* Just like finding friendships based on our interests, TGD people can also find belonging in groups that have nothing to do with identity, but are related to other things they care about.

* TGD communities can serve not only as a place to find belonging but also as a way to create positive social change.

* For this to happen, we all need to do our part to make sure our TGD communities are safe places for all. This means ensuring we aren't letting racism, sexism, ableism, or other harmful forces exist in our TGD spaces.

* By coming together with others, we have more power to create the social changes we need that will help TGD people, and others, feel belonging in more spaces.

CHAPTER 7

BUILDING A MEANINGFUL LIFE

Trying to get your parents to use the right pronouns for you, convincing your school to designate a gender-neutral bathroom, or avoiding more transphobic news on social media is probably not what gets you up in the morning. Some mornings you probably wonder why you're getting up at all. But the point of all of this, of resilience and this whole book, is to get the skills to stay strong in order to build a great life and one that is meaningful for you.

Being resilient involves not only surviving tough times but also bouncing forward toward a life that you really want. Part of resilience is also having a reason to stick around, get up in the morning, and keep building your future. That's why the final thing we would like to talk about in this book is building a meaningful life. Our sense of meaning and purpose can get us through even the most difficult situations. For example, in *Man's Search for Meaning*, Viktor Frankl (1992) writes about how even in concentration camps during the Holocaust, it was possible for people to survive by finding meaning in little things, helping others, imagining a better future, and connecting (even if only in their minds) with loved ones. Additionally, many people who have gone through tough times look back to realize that they grew as a result because they learned what was truly important to them.

We'll start by looking at ways people find meaning, including through discovering their values. We'll also talk about how these ways of finding meaning can relate to being a TGD person. Then we'll explore areas of meaning that may help you find important activities and experiences you want in your life. Using fictional stories drawn from our experiences and experiences of TGD people we know, we'll share some examples along the way and pose some questions to help you explore what can contribute to giving your life meaning and purpose.

WHAT IS MOST IMPORTANT TO YOU?

Different people have different answers to the question "What makes life meaningful?" And as we go through different times in life, we may find that our answers to this question change. Our identities may also help us understand how to make our lives meaningful. Below we describe some important areas that people find bring them meaning and purpose. We also talk about how being TGD brings opportunities to develop this sense of meaning.

Values

Discovering what is meaningful to you often starts with clarifying your values and then finding ways to live based on those values. Values are ways of being that feel important and right to you, not things you can get or accomplish. For example, we may value being kind, honest, creative, smart, silly, responsible, generous, adventurous, courageous, a hard worker, loyal, adaptable, curious, compassionate, friendly, funny, hopeful, or grateful. Which of these are most important to you? Do you have others not mentioned here? If you can't get ideas, search the web for "values sorting," and look for websites where you can do a values-sorting exercise. This will help you get more clarity about what does and doesn't matter to you. Maybe you'll surprise yourself with what you choose!

Knowing what your values are can help you turn toward what matters to you regardless of what your environment is. No one can take your values away from you, no matter what they think of you or do to you. Knowing this can give you a sense of meaning through any challenge. We recommend that you write down or do some creative piece on what values are important to you. You don't need to choose only the most important or grandest values, like peace or justice. Being playful, enjoying nature, being creative—these are all important values too.

Example: *Building a life based on valuing adventure and curiosity*

Leticia is a real explorer type. She feels like the meaning of life is to venture into new territories and see all there is to see. She doesn't feel very safe walking around where she lives, so she feels stuck. She decides to talk to her friend's dad about this. He recommends looking into what clubs are at school, to see if there is anything that might feel right. Leticia asks her guidance counselor if there are any school clubs that do adventurous things. Her guidance counselor says, "Oh yes! You should join the astronomy club." "Astronomy?" she says, skeptical. Her guidance counselor explains that the teacher of the astronomy club takes students on overnight trips outside of the city several times a year so they can be in dark places to see different planets and stars. Plus, if she joins the club, she can apply for scholarships to go to an astronaut camp over the summer. *This is amazing!* she thinks. Leticia has gone from feeling stuck to having something more than she thought was possible in just one day.

Update: Leticia went to astronaut camp and got to experience all sorts of new things there. Now she enjoys going out at night and looking at the stars and wondering about who and what else is out there. When she starts to feel anxious or worried about her future, or whether she can really be herself, she tries to focus on upcoming astronomy trips.

Building Your Future

One of the things that the youth we talked to said is that being able to imagine a future was a really important part of resilience for them. As a young person, you might not have control over your body, education, or what town you live in. You may be thinking about changes to your body or gendered appearance that aren't available to you yet. Or you might not be at a school that has a community of TGD people for you to connect with. It can be painful to have to wait to access these things and make the life you really want and need. But meanwhile, many youth share that imagining that world is really helpful. You may find it encouraging to learn more about the lives of happy, satisfied TGD people. You could read recent biographies of TGD people, follow some on social media, or listen to their podcasts. You might write about what you'd like for your life and how you see yourself in three, five, or even ten years. But meanwhile, there are things you can do to build a meaningful life right now, and also build toward your bright future.

Helping Others

While everyone wants to feel good themselves, many people can sense that somewhere deep inside, they also want to help others around them feel good. Research shows that even very small children will try to help others if they can (Brownell 2013). For example, you might have noticed that when someone around you drops a pen, you naturally tend to pick it up and give it back to them.

We often have a natural reaction to help others. We can do this on a small scale with something like picking up a pen, and we can do this on a larger scale, like starting an antibullying effort in our town. We can help the people we know and love, like checking on and listening to a friend who is going through a tough time. We can also help people we won't ever know, like volunteering to pack bags of food for people without homes. People who help others tend to end up feeling better themselves. Even more, people who are generous with helping others often find that more generous, kind people come into their lives. By being helpful, you're forming a strong community of people who will support you, as well.

But where should you start? Well, one place you could start is by asking those around you if they need help with anything. Does a parent need help cooking? Does a friend need help remembering their homework? Would a grandparent be happy if you called them to say hello? Have you searched online for volunteer events or groups in your area? These are also great ways to build community, make friends, and get more support from other people.

There are also ways TGD people can be especially helpful in certain situations. As many of you know, finding your gender, coming out, and expressing yourself in the world is not always an easy path. But because this path to knowing yourself is not easy, it can cause you to become wiser or stronger in some ways. If you have done some work to discover more about your identity, you can be a big help to other people who are just starting to explore who they are. For example, Dana Delgardo (2023) was a transgender man in the Air Force long before this was even permitted. He wrote about his experiences: "How did I cope with all those years of adversity? Like many others, I needed to help and give back." He started informally helping other trans people in the military navigate the systems. "My experience prior to being out helped me aid the survival of others...Aiding them gave my service additional meaning and helped my own sometimes-waning confidence."

Trust us that if you have gotten this far, there are plenty of others who could use your wisdom and experience. Just sharing your story or listening to someone else with kindness can be very important. Finding ways to be yourself, even in the face of minority stress, can support others who have marginalized identities to be themselves. You can inspire others inside and outside the TGD community by being yourself—even when it's not easy.

In fact, if you've had some hard times, these things can make it easier for you to help others. For example, understanding what feeling rejected for your identity feels like can allow you to better understand what it's like for people who have other marginalized identities and have also been rejected for their identities. Because of this understanding, you may be really excellent at helping to fight for fairness for all people. And you may discover that you feel more real kindness toward others who are experiencing hardship or need some help. We've noticed that many TGD youth get a lot out of offering to lead TGD groups, or LGBTQ+ school groups, or even moderating an TGD online group.

Whether you're volunteering, being a support to someone, or starting a movement, you can find ways to use your energy to help. Helping others can bring you a sense of meaning that makes it all worth it. So where should you start? You might begin by journaling about experiences you've had in the past where you were helpful to someone else, where someone else was helpful to you, or where you've seen or heard of someone else helping others. What types of actions seem most meaningful and inspiring to you? What fits with your values? Make sure to list the small things as well as the big things. We will talk more at the end of the chapter about how to turn some of these ideas into action.

Example: *Building a life that helps others*

Max feels like the most important thing he can do with his life is finding ways to help. Making friends is not so easy for him—people make him nervous and as a neurodivergent nonbinary person, he never quite feels like he knows how to fit in.

Max totally loves dogs. He really wants to do something where he gets to help dogs out. If he could make a friend along the way, that would be a bonus, but Max feels like he doesn't know where to begin. So the first step for Max is to talk to other people about his desire to help, and then write down some ideas. Max talks to parents, friends, and a teacher about his desire to figure out a way to be helpful to dogs and maybe meet people. One person tells him that sometimes there are volunteer dog walkers for older people who can no longer walk their dogs themselves. *That's it!* Max thinks. So now Max knows his big goal, but he still doesn't know how to make that happen. He decides his second step is finding other dog walkers he can talk to. Max asks people he knows with dogs and learns of two dog walkers he can talk to. He gets their contact information, then calls them and asks whether they would be willing to tell him whatever they think he needs to know about being a dog walker. Max learns about the rules at different parks and gets tips on how get started.

Now Max feels ready to do this. But how can he find the older people he would like to help? Max decides he needs to have some more conversations to find out how to get in touch with these people. Max talks again to some of his family, friends, and teachers. Based on their ideas, he decides he will make flyers to post near retirement homes, where there are a lot of older adults who might need some help with their dogs. He gets on his computer and puts down all of the important information on a flyer. Max has his mom look it over. He thinks it's ready to print, but his mom looks worried. She says she's too worried about him meeting people she doesn't know at their houses, so he cannot post these flyers. At first Max is very upset, but then he thinks, *Maybe this just means there is another step. I have to figure out a plan my mom and I can agree on.* Max talks with his mom about how they could make this work, and they agree that she'll come with him the first time he meets new people.

Max can finally post the flyers! After a few days he gets his first call. He follows the steps the other dog walkers recommended and is soon walking two dogs every day after school. Sometimes he calls one of the other dog walkers to see if they want to walk together, and it's easier because they always have a lot of things to talk about—dogs!

Update: Max now has a job working with dogs. He still volunteers for some of the same people and has become friends with some of the older adults he has met over time. He came out to some of them, and they seemed to think it was no big deal. Plus, he still meets up with his dog-walking friend and sometimes they help each other out if one is sick or away. Max feels good about his ability to help out both people and dogs, and he feels it brings a sense of meaning and purpose to his day, no matter how he's feeling otherwise.

Improving the World

Whether it's working with a group trying to get rights for TGD people, helping build better hiking trails in your area, joining a group that helps injured wildlife, or starting a LGBTQ+ support group at school, by joining an effort toward a better world, people often find a sense of meaning and purpose that can help them feel good about themselves and their lives. Putting our energy and time toward something larger that we care about can also bring us together with others who have similar interests and values, and this can make for great friendships!

Being TGD is pretty great in that you're already a part of making important social change. Many TGD people can feel a part of a larger effort to break down limiting gender beliefs. Since no one really fits the perfect man or woman image we have often been told is best, this can be an effort that involves and helps more than just TGD people. TGD people have historically been part of fighting for justice for other TGD people, and finding meaning through that.

Randi Robertson, a sixty-year-old trans woman who grew up in a very conservative religious family talked about how she found resilience: "We used to always say, 'It gets better.' It's a nice little flip phrase. But it gets better not because we sit and wait for it to get better. It gets better because we work at it, not just as individuals, but as communities. Not just as a marginal community, but as the community at large. It gets better because we invest in and work to make it get better" (Luterman 2023). In fact, many TGD youth have found themselves in leadership roles with other LGBTQ+ youth to change their school culture or policy when it comes to queer and trans students. TGD people who understand minority stress from their own lives can also feel part of an effort to fight for justice across all marginalized identities. Many TGD people are involved in efforts for TGD rights, antiracist work, environmentalism, disability justice, and other important projects. It may be that a TGD identity makes you more able to see and respond to injustices in the world. It can feel really good to be part of this effort for social change.

Being Part of Something Larger

From finding a spiritual path to connecting with nature, many people around the world find the sense that they're a part of something larger than themselves to be extremely meaningful and a big part of getting through tough times.

If you're a person who feels drawn to religious or spiritual life, that can be a powerful way to connect to other communities and find more meaning in your life. After all, billions of people follow one religion or another and still more identify as being spiritual. However, TGD people can find it hard to find a religious or spiritual community that is accepting and welcoming to TGD identities. Many TGD people who participated in religious activities growing up experienced hearing about or witnessing transphobia. The good news is that there are now so many ways to connect to religious or spiritual groups that are not only accepting but really welcoming of LGB and TGD people. Look for organizations that call themselves "LGBTQ+ welcoming" or "affirming." Look for welcoming statements on their website. If in doubt, email the religious leader of the group. If they're defensive or otherwise not helpful about your questions, this might not be the place for you.

There are many nonmainstream spiritual and religious groups and traditions as well. Nature-based traditions, new age traditions, or mindfulness groups, for example, might be a better fit for you. What's important is that the tradition helps you feel more connected to the wider world, matches your needs, and fits well with what you believe. It's also okay to not be sure what you believe, so check out a number of different traditions.

Lastly, there are so many books, podcasts, social media accounts, and websites that can help you explore your own pathways to a spiritual or religious life. There are quite a few that focus on LGBTQ+ identities in religion and spirituality. You can learn about the many, many ways others are spiritual or religious, and read their thoughts about it.

You may find meaning in being a part of something larger even when it isn't part of an organized tradition. Many people find this meaning when they connect to the natural world. If this is you, you might want to learn more about the natural world and spend time in it. Volunteering or getting a job that lets you connect with wildlife, ecology, or nature might be a great way to ensure you're able to connect regularly.

Creativity

Many people find meaning through becoming more creative. Part of the beauty of our lives is our ability to create music, art, writing, dance, and even gardening or cooking. What are you drawn to create?

We don't need a reason to create other than that it's a part of what we want to do. When we feel a strong emotion, whether positive or negative, it can be a really great time to create something with that energy or feeling. Creating has given many artists, dancers, writers, and chefs a sense of meaning and purpose in life.

Sometimes people of marginalized identities are able to create in special ways because of all the difficult things they have had to feel and understand in their lives. For example, African American spiritual music, jazz, and the blues are types of music that show the resilience of enslaved Blacks in America. The people who created this music found ways to express their profound hardship through inspiring music that has influenced most of American music ever since. TGD people of all cultures have creative gifts to share with the world. In this way, creating can give us a sense of meaning as well as a chance to connect with communities of other creative people and TGD people.

Remember, you don't need to be especially good or talented at something to do it. It takes a lot of practice to become good, and even if you never do, you can still be creative. There are many craft nights, dance groups, and music groups that are designed for beginners and people who are just trying things out. Some well-known smartphone companies offer free classes on creative activities, like drawing, photography, and making music on your phone or tablet. There are literally thousands of craft, art, music, cooking, and dance ideas on social media. We encourage you to avoid self-criticism when you try to be creative and just do what feels good for you.

Example: *Building a life around creativity*

Jian lives to be creative. Although they have loved dancing ever since they were a young child, they only really dance in their room. They watch videos online and learn the moves. They're afraid to take a dance class because it seems like only cisgender girls go there, and they don't think they'll be accepted. But they love dance so much that they don't want to let anything stand in their way. So Jian knows they want to find a place where they can take dance lessons and feel safe.

Jian decides their first step will be researching what dance schools are close to their home. They go online and find five dance schools. A few of the classes they see listed look like they would be really awesome! Jian decides they should talk to their grandma first, to see whether she would pay for Jian to take dance classes. Jian's grandma says that she can afford two of the schools. Now Jian knows they have to take the next step, which they have been fearing. They need to call both dance schools to see what they say about having nonbinary students in their classes. To protect themself, Jian decides they will not tell the schools their name when they call for the first time. Also, Jian knows that they might feel terrible if someone says something harmful to them on the phone, so they decide to ask a friend to be there with them.

At the first school they call, the person who picks up the phone doesn't know what nonbinary is and seems to get awkward. Jian and their friend decide to take a break before calling the next place. After a walk and a snack, they feel better and get up the courage to call the next school. Jian is very relieved when the person who answers their call says that they have other nonbinary students at that dance school and they should feel safe there. As soon as Jian hangs up, they aren't sure. They still feel nervous to go because they're afraid of what the other kids will be like. But Jian's friend says, "It's okay. I'm going to ask my mom if I can go too. Will you go if I go?" Jian is glad they asked their friend to be there!

Update: Jian no longer feels nervous about going and is totally loving the dance classes. Their friend didn't continue coming, but they have met some new friends there. They have been in two performances and feel these have been some of the highlights of their life.

Enjoying Life to the Fullest

Another way that some people find meaning is simply in enjoying life as much as possible. Some people find it most important to just appreciate and be grateful for all the beauty and amazing things they encounter. Enjoying life like this doesn't mean these people need to do big, special things all the time, and it doesn't mean doing only pleasurable things, like eating, using alcohol, or being sexual. Instead, enjoying life to the fullest means that while you're living your regular life, you take time to appreciate and be grateful for what you experience. The great thing here is that you can literally fit this into your life at any time. Instead of rushing through life trying to do all the things on your list, you take time to spend with people you love. Maybe you go out for a walk at sunset to see the colors, or you explore that new place you've been wanting to visit. You might really enjoy listening to music or going to see a dance performance. Sometimes it's even as simple as paying enough attention to enjoy the feeling of a hot shower or of the sun on your skin. We think of it as making simple moments special, but also making some extraspecial moments. For example, noticing a cute dog on your way to school and taking a few minutes to pet the dog (with the owner's permission) can make your walk special. But throwing a surprise picnic for your friend's birthday might be an extraspecial moment that makes your life feel better overall.

TGD people often feel left out of those big, special moments that are always on TV or in movies. Weddings, first dates, coming-of-age traditions ("becoming a man" or "becoming a woman"), prom, or even sports can feel pretty far out of reach. Even getting your driver's license means having to choose what gender marker to put on your license. But as it turns out, those big, special moments are only a little part of enjoying life to the fullest. As it turns out, where most people find the greatest satisfaction is in the little moments that happen every day. Taking time each day to stop and make a special moment for yourself can help ensure that you have that pleasure. You can also make extraspecial moments for yourself. Throw a queer prom for yourself and others so you have the prom you've always wanted. Have your own license ceremony where you and your best friend celebrate being able to drive (even if the gender marker doesn't fit for you). Reclaim special moments so they work for you.

Taking On a (Little or Big) Challenge

Some people view life as a series of challenges and opportunities that can help them grow. Life can be a journey of growing to be stronger, wiser, more compassionate toward yourself and others, of discovering your special talents, and of developing different abilities. We're always growing in new ways, whether we're going through an easy time or a hard time. For that reason, focusing our lives on learning and growing can be a great way to find a sense of meaning.

Challenges can be big or small, long or short. A lot of research shows that taking on even little challenges can help us feel a sense of control over our lives, improve our mood, and make life more worthwhile (Ryan and Deci 2017). You might have realized this after doing something that was just a little hard for you. Pushing yourself gently to try something new, to get better at something, or to try to get really good at something can give you that "I can do it!" feeling, which can carry through to the rest of your life.

Example: *Building a life around challenge*

Meriq likes fashion a lot. She decides it would be awesome to learn to make some of her own clothes, but she has no idea how to start. She realizes she can just sew patches onto some of her clothes, and soon she has saved enough to get studs and spikes she can add to her bag and jacket. This works pretty well, so she decides to push herself a little more and ask her grandma if she could use the sewing machine. Grandma shows her a few things, and it's really hard at first. Meriq messes up a lot of things before she can make a cute skirt out of vintage fabric that her grandma had said she could use. She's so proud of this skirt and every time some says, "Whoa, you made that?" she feels excited.

Rafael loves going to the gym. They feel like being more muscular helps them look more masculine. But they have been feeling kind of depressed and down lately. After seeing a video on a different way to lift weights that might help increase their strength, they check it out with a few friends who lift. When their friends agree that it seems safe, they decide to give themselves a minichallenge: they'll try this new way of working out for one month and see how it goes. In their phone they keep a note of all of the exercises and how much weight they were able to lift. They feel satisfied every time they're able to do a little more, and when they're feeling down, they look at their numbers to remind themselves that they can try new things.

Marcus plays guitar and is okay at it. She really enjoys playing, but mostly just messes around. She wants to get better at a certain song by a band that's coming into town, but she can't keep her focus. She decides to let herself buy a ticket to their concert only after she learns the song. After a few days she notices it's sounding pretty good. She records it and adds it to the background of a video she posted and buys herself the ticket.

As you might be picking up, all of these things involve a few steps. First is finding a reachable goal. You're not going to feel good about yourself if you decide to become a professional dancer by Wednesday and you've never danced before! Second is chunking it out into simple steps. If you want to get really good at playing your guitar, make your first small goal getting good at one song, or learning one new chord a week. Third is to give yourself a little reward (especially if you can't get going) for achieving the small steps and the big challenge. This could be something you buy for yourself, like tickets or a coffee, something you get to do, like watching a movie or seeing a friend, or it could be getting to show off your results. For this reason, we recommend you ensure you have an actual product at the end to admire. This could be a recording of your song or your new skirt like in the examples. We think that using your journal to write down your accomplishments is a great idea. Or it could be just noticing that you're stronger, telling a friend about your achievement, or even making a video of yourself to post on social media. But having something you can use to admire your accomplishments goes a long way! Be sure to go back to look at what you accomplished and remind yourself how hard you worked.

Doing this can be very useful for TGD people because so much of your life can be spent feeling like you're "less than" other people. Things that cisgender kids get admired for, like being pretty or handsome, might feel out of reach to you. Playing sports might feel awkward. Decisions about your body, identity, and life might be mostly out of your control. So if you're constantly thinking, I can't do it, making your own challenges and building your sense of I can do it is amazing! Plus, then you're growing your life in ways that are meaningful and important to you. Trying to push yourself out of your comfort zone a little to accomplish something is a way to guide your life in the direction you want.

You can also consider how to combine this with other things you want to do. If you're trying to expand your community, maybe your challenge is to join three new online groups and post a hello message on each one. If you're trying to be better friends with your body, maybe your challenge is to enjoy fifteen minutes of fun movement a day for a week. Just remember to reward yourself for trying and accomplishing your goals. And, if you can't do it, don't beat yourself up. Just set a more achievable goal next time.

TAKING ACTION

Once you have a better idea of what feels meaningful to you, you can take steps toward building a life that puts the most important things up front and center. And you don't have to choose just one thing from the areas you've read about. You can have lots of different things in your life that contribute to making life feel meaningful. Bringing what we find to be most important into our lives can be done by setting larger goals, and then breaking down those goals into smaller steps that we can do one at a time. This helps big goals to not feel overwhelming or impossible.

Now that you have seen a few examples of how people bring meaning into their lives, it's your turn. What areas that we've talked about seemed most meaningful to you—helping others, being a part of something larger, creativity, enjoying life to the fullest, becoming your best self? Are there certain values that are most important to you? Spend some time journaling about what sounded most inspiring to you and why.

Next, it can be helpful to explore what actions you might take to build parts of your life around the things you have discovered to be most mean-ingful. You can start by coming up with a whole bunch of ideas, even if they seem impossible. For example, if you really feel it's important to contribute to a better world, and you really feel a spiritual connection to nature, what could that look like in action? In your journal, write down all of the options. Here are a few of ours:

- volunteering with a group to collect trash from beaches

- setting up bird houses

- organizing a letter-writing campaign for an environmental cause and inviting friends to join

- asking the leaders in your culture how you can help restore the traditional lands of your culture

You might keep adding to the list for a week or two; different things you see on social media or talk to people about give you even more ideas. It's important to write the ideas down even if they seem impossible, because you might find simpler versions that are possible.

Once you have your list, you can then highlight any that really moti-vate you. The next step is to find ways that you can get involved in those things that work for your life. For example, your author Ry loves birds. He would love to help take care of wild birds. Sometimes he wishes he was a veterinarian for birds! But even though he's not a veterinarian, he has found smaller ways he can help birds. One way he finds ideas for getting involved with birds is by telling a lot of people of his interest. Sometimes he finds out that the person he's talking to knows of an organization he can get involved with. For example, one year Ry learned about an international parrot conservation organization and volunteered with them. Another year, he was googling bird rescues near where he lives and found a hospital for songbirds where he could help with preparing the birds' food. Both times, Ry was able to feel good about being involved in something meaningful. As a bonus, he met and became friendly with other people who also cared about birds.

See if you can find actions you might take that relate to the larger effort you care about. What smaller actions can you take that relate to the bigger things you care about? Try a few things and see what feels good. If it feels a bit unsafe or scary to enter a new community of people involved in the efforts you care about, you can turn back to chapter 6 on community connection, and use some of the tips there on finding communities to make that process feel safer.

Putting what brings you meaning front and center in life makes it a lot easier to handle minority stress and any other challenges life throws your way. As you start living a life based on what brings you meaning and purpose, you might find that tough times are easier when you think about these things that really matter to you. When you start to think that you'd be better off just staying in bed for the day, you can think about what you care most about, and focus on orienting yourself toward that, even if it just means starting small. For example, on a hard day, someone who likes to help others could try sending out a prayer that other TGD people know there is nothing wrong with them and find happiness in their day. This small action can be helpful and turn them back toward what motivates them in this life.

TAKEAWAYS

✱ Having something that gives us meaning and purpose can help us be resilient by giving us something to focus on and do that feels important.

✱ These are some common areas where people find meaning and purpose:

* Values

* Building a future

* Helping others

* Improving the world

* Creativity

* Enjoying life to the fullest

* Taking on a challenge

✱ Once you know what ways feel important for you in finding meaning and purpose, you can discover actions that link to these things by generating ideas based on what you see or hear about others doing, even if those things feel too big or impossible for you; and by figuring out smaller action steps that you're able to do that relate to these bigger ideas.

✱ When you're feeling down, returning to what brings you meaning, and finding even a small way to do something related to that, can support your resilience.

CLOSING

We're so excited that we have been able to join you on this journey of building resilience and creating a meaningful life. In the beginning of this book, we talked about how social changes are needed so that simply existing as a TGD person will no longer require resilience. However, even with things as they are, we hope to empower ourselves and each other to stand strong against any forces that aim to stifle us. We can do this by giving ourselves the resources to be as resilient as we can and building lives of meaning.

We wouldn't have written this book if we didn't believe that it was possible for you to keep making your life better and better. And when young people like you are able to do this, your success helps and inspires other TGD youth. Thank you for being a part of this inspiring group of people who keep walking through the tough stuff and staying open to not just surviving, but also to finding meaning, joy, and community. See you on the forward bounce!

RESOURCES

At http://www.newharbinger.com/54193, you'll find worksheets, handouts, and lists of resources, including books, social media accounts, and podcasts. We've listed these two resources here because we want you to have some safety information for easy reference. Keep these numbers in your phone for yourself or for a friend who is struggling.

The Trevor Project is especially for LGBTQ+ youth who are having thoughts or worries about suicide. You can text them, call them, or chat with them online 24/7. Go to https://www.thetrevorproject.org/get-help or call 1-866-488-7386 . We strongly recommend that all of our readers go to the Trevor Project page even if you're feeling great. Remember, even if you don't need their resources and information, you may have a friend who does.

The Trans Lifeline is a hotline staffed by trans/nonbinary people who are there to talk, even if you're not in a crisis. You can reach them at 1-877-565-8860. They aren't available 24/7 but they have great resources on their page: https://www.translifeline.org.

GLOSSARY

Affirmative care: Supportive and respectful care that recognizes and validates your individual gender identity

Affirmative medical care: Medical treatment that helps a person feel better in their gender identity

Allies: Supportive people who help and advocate for others

Binary gender: Having a gender that is "man" or "woman" (including trans people who identify this way)

Cisgender: People whose gender identity matches the sex they were assigned at birth (not transgender or nonbinary)

Coping: Ways to deal with stress or difficult feelings

Discrimination: When people are treated unfairly or differently based on something about them that they cannot change like race, gender, ability, or religion

Gender: A person's identity as a man, woman, both, neither, or a combination

Gender diverse: Anyone who is transgender, nonbinary, or has gender which is different from their gender at birth

Gender dysphoria: Unhappiness or dissatisfaction with how your body looks or how you're perceived by others related to your gender

Gender euphoria: Feeling happy, joyful, or content with your gender expression

Gender expression: How you express your gender with how you look, act, etc.

Gratitude: Feeling thankful for something

Grounding: Techniques to help you stay focused and calm in the moment

Human rights: Basic rights and freedoms that belong to every person

Internalized stigma: Messages you have started to believe from the culture around you that your marginalized identity is bad, gross, wrong, or otherwise less than other identities

Internalized transphobia: See "internalized stigma"

Intrinsic: Something that comes from inside you, like personal values, interests, or goals that are important to you, rather than things that come from outside, like money or fame

Invalidation: When someone ignores or doesn't take your feelings seriously, making you feel like your thoughts or experiences don't matter

LGBTQ+: An initialism that stands for lesbian, gay, bisexual, transgender, queer, or questioning, and more

Marginalized identities: Identities that are often treated badly or unfairly by others

Mindfulness: Paying attention to the present moment without judging your thoughts or feelings

Minority stress: Stress people feel related to their marginalized identity (like being trans, nonbinary, or gender diverse)

Misgendering: Referring to someone using the wrong gender pronouns or terms

Nonaffirmation: Similar to invalidation: not supporting or recognizing someone's identity

Nonbinary: Gender identities that are not male or female

Oppression: Unfair or cruel treatment of people or groups, especially based on factors like race, gender, or beliefs, that limits their rights or opportunities

Passing: Being seen by others as a certain gender

Prejudices: Biases or unfair opinions about certain groups of people

Racism: Prejudice based on race

Regulation: Making feelings or emotions less intense

Resilience: The ability to survive and thrive even when life is hard

Self-care: Actions that you do to make sure that your mind and body stay healthy

Self-harm: Hurting yourself on purpose, usually to try and cope with emotional pain

Sexual health: Taking care of your body and emotions related to relationships, puberty, sex, and sexual feelings

Socioeconomic: Referring to how money and social status affect people's lives

Spiritual self-care: Practices that nurture a sense of peace, meaning, or connection to something larger than oneself

Stressors: Things that cause stress or worry, like schoolwork, problems with friends, or family problems

TGD: An initialism that stands for trans and gender diverse

Toxic environments: Situations that are harmful to you either emotionally or physically

Transgender: An identity or description of someone who now identifies differently from the gender they were given at birth

Trans: An abbreviation for "transgender"

Trans man: A man who was assigned female at birth

Trans woman: A woman who was assigned male at birth

Trauma: The upset that results from an event that causes a severe threat to your safety and maybe even your life or other people's lives; it may result in high levels of emotional, psychological, and physical distress that can make it hard to feel okay, hopeful, or safe, day to day

Transphobia: Fear or dislike of TGD people; discrimination against TGD people

Well-being: The state of feeling good or healthy

REFERENCES

Breslow, A. S., M. E. Brewster, B. L. Velez, S. Wong, E. Geiger, and B. Soderstrom. 2015. "Resilience and Collective Action: Exploring Buffers Against Minority Stress for Transgender Individuals." *Psychology of Sexual Orientation and Gender Diversity* 2(3): 253.

Brownell, C. A. 2013. "Early Development of Prosocial Behavior: Current Perspectives." *Infancy* 18(1): 1–9.

Chödrön, P. 2001. *Tonglen: The Path of Transformation*. Halifax, Nova Scotia: Vajradhatu Publications.

Clond, M. 2016. "Emotional Freedom Techniques for Anxiety: A Systematic Review with Meta-Analysis." *The Journal of Nervous and Mental Disease* 204(5): 388–395.

Delgardo, D. 2023. "A Trans Man in the Military." In *Surviving Transphobia*, edited by L. A. Jacobs. London: Jessica Kingsley Publishers.

Dolan-Sandrino, G. 2017. "Transgender Kids Are Resilient. We Won't Let Trump Keep Us Down." *The Washington Post*, March 2. Retrieved September 14, 2023, from https://www.washingtonpost.com/posteverything/wp/2017/03/02 /transgender-kids-are-resilient-we-wont-let-trump-keep-us-down.

Drucker, Z. 2018. "Trans Icon Miss Major: 'We've Got to Reclaim Who the Fuck We Are.'" *Vice*, November 21. https://www.vice.com/en/article/j5z58d /miss-major-griffin-gracy-transgender-survival-guide.

Frankl, V. E. 1992. *Man's Search for Meaning: An Introduction to Logotherapy*, 4th ed. Boston: Beacon Press.

Goffnett, J., and M. S. Paceley. 2020. "Challenges, Pride, and Connection: A Qualitative Exploration of Advice Transgender Youth Have for Other Transgender Youth." *Journal of Gay & Lesbian Social Services* 32(3): 328–353.

Hanh, T. N. 2010. "Oprah Talks to Thich Nhat Hanh." Interview by Oprah Winfrey. https://www.oprah.com/spirit/oprah-talks-to-thich-nhat-hanh.

Hyatt, C. S., C. E. Sleep, J. Lamkin, J. L. Maples-Keller, C. Sedikides, W. Keith Campbell, and J. D. Miller. 2018. "Narcissism and Self-Esteem: A Nomological Network Analysis." *PloS One* 13(8): e0201088.

Institute of Medicine. 2005. *Dietary Reference Intakes for Water, Potassium, Sodium, Chloride, and Sulfate.* Washington, DC: National Academies Press.

Langer, S. J. 2019. *Theorizing Transgender Identity for Clinical Practice: A New Model for Understanding Gender.* Philadelphia: Jessica Kingsley Publishers.

Liska, D., E. Mah, T. Brisbois, P. L. Barrios, L. B. Baker, and L. L. Spriet. 2019. "Narrative Review of Hydration and Selected Health Outcomes in the General Population." *Nutrients* 11(1): 70.

Luterman, S. 2023. "'You've Got to Live Your Truth': Two Trans Elders on What Resistance and Resilience Mean to Them." *The 19th News*, June 26. https://19thnews.org/2023/06/trans-elders-resistance-resilience-pride-month.

Lorde, A. 1988. *A Burst of Light and Other Essays.* New York: Kitchen Table: Women of Color Press.

Manyena, S. B., G. O'Brien, P. O'Keefe, and J. Rose. 2011. "Disaster Resilience: A Bounce Back or Bounce Forward Ability." *Local Environment* 5: 417–424.

Maslow, A. H. 1943. "A Theory of Human Motivation." *Psychological Review* 50(4): 370–396.

Menakem, R. 2017. *My Grandmother's Hands: Racialized Trauma and the Pathway to Mending Our Hearts and Bodies.* Las Vegas, NV: Central Recovery Press.

Neff, K. D. 2011. "Self-Compassion, Self-Esteem, and Well-Being." *Social and Personality Psychology Compass* 5(1): 1–12.

———. 2021. *Fierce Self-Compassion: How Women Can Harness Kindness to Speak Up, Claim Their Power and Thrive.* New York: HarperCollins.

Neff, K. D., and P. McGehee. 2009. "Self-Compassion and Psychological Resilience Among Adolescents and Young Adults." *Self and Identity* 9(3): 225–40.

Neff, K. D., and R. Vonk. 2009. "Self-Compassion Versus Global Self-Esteem: Two Different Ways of Relating to Oneself." *Journal of Personality* 77(1): 23–50.

Paceley, M. S., J. Goffnett, A. L. Diaz, S. K. Kattari, J. Navarro, and E. Greenwood. 2021. "I Didn't Come Here to Make Trouble: Resistance Strategies Utilized by Transgender and Gender Diverse Youth in the Midwestern US." *Youth* 1(1): 29–46.

Roth, G. 1998. *When You Eat at the Refrigerator, Pull Up a Chair: 50 Ways to Feel Thin, Gorgeous, and Happy (When You Feel Anything But)*. New York: Hachette Books.

Ryan, R. M., and E. L. Deci. 2017. *Self-Determination Theory: Basic Psychological Needs in Motivation, Development, and Wellness*. New York: Guilford.

Singh, A. A. 2013. "Transgender Youth of Color and Resilience: Negotiating Oppression and Finding Support." *Sex Roles* 68: 690–702.

Stetter, F., and S. Kupper. 2002. "Autogenic Training: A Meta-Analysis of Clinical Outcome Studies." *Applied Psychophysiology and Biofeedback* 27: 45–98.

Tedeschi, R. G., and L. G. Calhoun. 2004. "Posttraumatic Growth: Conceptual Foundations and Empirical Evidence." *Psychological Inquiry* 15(1): 1–18.

Testa, R. J., D. Coolhart, and J. L. Peta. 2019. *The Gender Quest Workbook: A Guide for Teens and Young Adults Exploring Gender Identity*. Oakland, CA: New Harbinger Publications.

Vigna, A. J., J. Poehlmann-Tynan, and B. W. Koenig. 2018. "Does Self-Compassion Facilitate Resilience to Stigma? A School-Based Study of Sexual And Gender Minority Youth." *Mindfulness* 9(3): 914–924.

Jayme L. Peta, PhD, is a psychologist with clinical and research experience in improving health and wellness for trans and nonbinary youth and adults. Currently, Peta is faculty at the Wright Institute, and has published articles and chapters on the experiences of LGBTQ+ people in crisis and public mental health settings. Peta is also a trainer with the LGBTQ+ Clinical Academy, which provides in-depth training in LGBTQ+-affirming therapy and cultural competence for public and community mental health providers in the San Francisco Bay Area.

Deb Coolhart, PhD, LMFT, is a licensed marriage and family therapist in private practice, and associate professor in the Syracuse University marriage and family therapy program. For twenty-five years, her clinical and scholarly work has focused on the strengths and challenges of trans people and their loved ones, and she has published several journal articles and book chapters on providing gender-affirmative care to trans and nonbinary people and their families. Twenty years ago, Coolhart created a clinical team of master's students who work specifically with trans clients, their partners, and their families in a free university clinic—providing a valuable service to the transgender community in Central New York, including providing letters of support for gender-affirming medical treatments.

Rylan Jay Testa, PhD, is a clinical psychologist and transgender man. He has served as an assistant professor, researcher, clinical supervisor, consultant, and trainer in the areas of trans and nonbinary mental health and resilience for over a decade. Testa now concentrates his efforts on healing and transformative clinical work, integrating psychospiritual and nature-based healing modalities. Testa's work aims to support the inherent resilience of all life that is available in each of us, rooted in our authentic diversity of bodies, identities, experiences, and expressions.

More ⏱️ Instant Help Books for Teens

An Imprint of New Harbinger Publications

THE GENDER QUEST WORKBOOK

A Guide for Teens and Young Adults Exploring Gender Identity

978-1626252974 / US $22.95

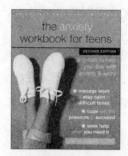

THE ANXIETY WORKBOOK FOR TEENS, SECOND EDITION

Activities to Help You Deal with Anxiety and Worry

978-1684038633 / US $21.95

OVERCOMING SUICIDAL THOUGHTS FOR TEENS

CBT Activities to Reduce Pain, Increase Hope, and Build Meaningful Connections

978-1684039975 / US $18.95

THE BULLYING WORKBOOK FOR TEENS

Activities to Help You Deal with Social Aggression and Cyberbullying

978-1608824502 / US $22.95

JUST AS YOU ARE

A Teen's Guide to Self-Acceptance and Lasting Self-Esteem

978-1626255906 / US $17.95

FIND YOUR SELF-LOVE HERE

A Creative Journal to Help Teens Build Confidence and Embrace Who They Are

978-1648482922 / US $19.95

🌱 new**harbinger**publications

1-800-748-6273 / newharbinger.com

(VISA, MC, AMEX / prices subject to change without notice)   Follow Us 📷 👍 ✖ ▶ 📌 in ♪ ⓖ

Don't miss out on new books from New Harbinger.
Subscribe to our email list at **newharbinger.com/subscribe** 🖱️

Did you know there are **free tools** you can download for this book?

Free tools are things like **worksheets, guided meditation exercises**, and **more** that will help you get the most out of your book.

You can download free tools for this book—whether you bought or borrowed it, in any format, from any source—from the New Harbinger website. All you need is a NewHarbinger.com account. Just use the URL provided in this book to view the free tools that are available for it. Then, click on the "download" button for the free tool you want, and follow the prompts that appear to log in to your NewHarbinger.com account and download the material.

You can also save the free tools for this book to your **Free Tools Library** so you can access them again anytime, just by logging in to your account! Just look for this button on the book's free tools page.

+ Save this to my free tools library

If you need help accessing or downloading free tools, visit **newharbinger.com/faq** or contact us at **customerservice@newharbinger.com**.